The Unscheduled Stops

Sinead MacDughlas

Print Edition

ISBN # 978-0-9878618-2-5

This is a work of fiction. All characters are fictitious and any resemblance to person, alive or dead, is purely coincidental.

All images in this book, aside from the cover art images, were obtained from the public domain, under licence cc 1.0
All images, excepting cover designs, (copyright noted), and the image on Pages 142 and the dedication, are of Union Station, in Toronto, Ontario Canada.

CONTENTS

** Not found in the free digital edition

For Dave, Ian, Becky and Carolyn; four true friends who know the station well, and all the best stops.

They also know the worst, yet they never hesitate to hop aboard.

All Aboard!

When once asked by a friend, to describe the way I think, I struggled with several possible analogies. Finally, I blurted out, "Union Station!"

"What?" my wide-eyed friend asked.

"Union Station…in Toronto. Have you ever been there?"

"Uuuuuh huuuuh?" The response was accompanied by a single cocked eyebrow and a sideways stare, her mouth pursed.

"My brain is like the station." I told her to picture each person in the station as a thought headed for a certain destination. Each train is a subject of those thoughts. The train for "Home" might have thoughts jumping on or off at Dusting, Children, Laundry, Dinner, Hubby, etc. Sometimes, the train "Work" train would have a few passengers headed for stops at Customers, Paycheque, Break-time, Co-workers, etc. A train called "Errands" has stops at Groceries, Dry Cleaner, Oil Change…and the list goes on. I always have several trains running at once, with several hundred thoughts jumping on and off at different locations.

Then there are the random thoughts. These are like the people who wander around the station, kind of lost, no clear destination in mind until they hop on one of the trains. These thoughts often jump off the trains in the strangest places, completely unscheduled stops. They are my muses. I write them down whenever I have an opportunity. They become my poems, characters and short stories.

Of all the processes, constantly in action at the little "Union Station" in my head, those Unscheduled Stops are some of my favourites. I hope you'll enjoy them too...

P.S. I've included three additional short stories and one free-write, that aren't available in the digital edition of "The Unscheduled Stops," as well as first chapter samples of two novels, and two novellas. After all, if you've been generous enough to purchase the printed book, I can certainly provide you with more than the free e-book contains. Thank you.

Sin

Daisy's Love at War

"Daisy's Love at War" is a short story I wrote for the many wonderful people who follow my Facebook fan page. It was inspired by a story my Grandmother told me about an old beau of hers, who was killed in action during World War Two. When going through her belongings, after she passed away, I stumbled across a photo of a young man in uniform. There was no label to tell me who this man was, and there were no other pictures of him anywhere. My imagination was stirred by the mysterious photo. Thinking it might be a picture of the young soldier she'd told me about, I began to wonder...what might have happened "if"...

"When did I get so old?" Daisy Patterson's raspy voice startled me out of my daydream. I looked up from the sheaf of papers in my lap, to study the tiny, wrinkled creature propped up in the bed across the room. "Pardon me, Daisy?"

"I was so young yesterday!" she said, her dark-brown eyes twinkling merrily. It was going to be one of her better days. There were days when her dementia had her huddled in dark subway tunnels, where muffled explosions made the ground shudder, and we couldn't reach her. At other times, she would descend into childhood nightmares of whiskey-reeking monsters with brutal fists and wingless angels scented with vanilla-roses. Some days she became the blushing bride, or young mother, full of loving pride.

Once in a very little while, she was the bustling matron, crooning over her new granddaughter.

Today, she was someone else; someone I had yet to meet.

I enjoyed my time at the nursing home and had for the five years I'd been volunteering there. Once a month I settled in the common room to read to those who had decided to join my little circle. Each time we'd draw a name from a hat. The winner selected the reading for the day, whether it was an article from a magazine, a chapter of a favourite book, or a short story someone had come across in the resident's library. Once a week, I came by just to have tea and chat, or console someone through trying times.

I'd been with Daisy when they told her Charlie, her husband, had passed away.

"Oh no, you're mistaken," The young bride persona had chirped. "Why he just rang five minutes ago to say he'd be home in time for tea."

"Young, so young and so in love. He was my world, you know?"

Sometimes I thought the dementia must be a blessing. Daisy hadn't been lucid when her son and his family had been killed by a drunk driver, seven years ago. She was far from aware when her husband of fifty-eight years dropped dead from heatstroke, while raking leaves in their little yard, during an Indian summer. She'd already been living in her world of memory and fantasy for years by then. She also hadn't had a visitor, aside from her pastor or

4

myself, in the three years since Charlie's passing.

Today was a visiting day. I'd been reading to Daisy from her favourite story. It was typed, double-spaced, on one hundred and two wrinkled sheets of yellowed, legal-sized paper. There was no author's name or title. Almost a book, it was a love story, written in the form of letters between a soldier and his girlfriend during the Second World War.

The story was well-written, in plain language, and full of emotion: loss, fear, longing. Two distinct voices spoke from the pages. Since lucid conversation with Daisy was rare, I usually spent my visits to her reading aloud. Whenever Daisy's name came out of the hat at Reading Circle, she invariably chose a few pages from this pile.

I'd asked Charlie about it once, before he'd passed. He said she'd dug it out of the bottom of their hope-chest one day, not long before she'd come to the home. Of all her belongings, the story was one she wouldn't leave behind. Daisy, it seems, had been an avid writer in her youth. She'd even published a few of her stories in literary magazines. Charlie said he'd never read it. He assumed she'd written the story while he was away at war. Left with his family here in Canada, a young war-bride deposited on the Patterson's dairy farm; writing had been her solace.

"He was so handsome in his uniform." she sighed.

"Yes, Charlie was a striking man." I agreed absently, scanning the next page.

"Charlie?" the incredulity in her voice yanked my attention

from the papers.

"Charlie looked like a dressed ape in his uniform! I used to tease that they'd kept him off the front lines because he'd boost the morale of the Nazis if they thought the rest of the army was as shabby." A gravelly laugh followed, but the twinkle was still there.

"No, dearie, it was Andrew who looked so dashing in his battle-dress. He was tall then, my Andrew: tall, and slim and strong as a draft horse. He had the voice of an angel—in spite of that atrocious Canadian accent—and the eyes of the devil himself..." her voice faded away. Had her eyes been closed, I'd have sworn she'd fallen asleep. "Bottle-glass green..." she croaked quietly after a long pause, "with little specks of blue. His face was strong and sharp, but you'd hardly notice for his eyes. He was such a charmer." She sounded so young, so wistful.

"Your beau before you met Charlie?" I asked gently. Andrew was the name of the man in the story. I wondered if it was the senility talking now. Perhaps she'd read it so many times, her story had become real to her.

"Somewhat." Daisy tittered cryptically. She sounded like a teenage girl with a piece of juicy gossip. "He had a lot of girls, my Andrew, but I was his best girl. He'd give us all pets and kisses, but only I got letters. I'd have married him if he'd asked, but the war took him away," wistful again, and sad.

I'd never made it to the end of the story; Daisy preferred the first half to the last. Apparently, it was a romantic tragedy.

"Was he killed?"

"Yes…" she was silent for a moment, staring out the window behind me into her memories. "But he came back for me despite that. Death couldn't keep him away."

"I don't understand."

"No, you wouldn't…" She fidgeted a little in the bed, pulling herself up to sit straighter. She reminded me of my own granny, who would adopt the same posture, just before she began to lecture me about some topic she was passionate about. I put the sheaf of papers down on the tea table beside me, giving her my undivided attention. Sometimes the best gift you could offer the residents was a sympathetic and attentive ear. Many of them had such wonderful stories to share.

"Andrew was a flying officer in the Royal Canadian Air Force. We met in London when he was on a leave. He was so charming; I couldn't help but fall in love with him." I knew much of this from the pages I'd read to her so often but, as any true story-teller, she would ensure the tale was complete. "I wasn't the only one, though. All the girls loved 'Dandy-Andy'. I only had two weeks to make myself his best girl. I was considered a bit of a beauty in those days...Andrew was mine in four days. He flirted with the other girls, but I knew it was me he was coming back for when the war was over."

"I cried when he shipped out, of course; all the girls did. He promised to write me a letter every day, and he kept his promise. Andrew was a great writer, much better than I ever was. Sometimes his letters would come in bundles, having waited

somewhere for days and weeks before they could be delivered."
Her usual frailty had fallen away as she spoke; her voice stronger
and more passionate than I'd ever heard.

"He was so proud to be chosen for Dieppe. He wrote me the
day before they deployed. It was weeks before I had another letter.
This time it was taped to a parcel, from his brother. Andrew's
plane had been shot down. He was presumed...dead." Her breath
hitched, the last word coming out in a nearly inaudible whisper.

"His brother, Tommy, only mailed the package because his
bunk-mates had sent his belongings to the family, and they'd found
our letters. Inside the box he'd shipped, was a small bundle of
letters Andrew had written for me. They'd never made it to the
post. A second bundle contained every letter I'd ever written him."

"I cried for weeks. I mourned my Andrew the way so many
other women mourned their husbands, brothers and sons; with fear,
anger, hope and pain, all wrapped up in hatred for the Nazis and
pride for our brave men." There were tears in her eyes even now,
suspended there by nothing more than her apparent refusal to
release them.

"I lived most of the rest of the war like a young widow;
martyring myself in the hospitals, volunteering wherever help was
needed. I took a job as a typist. I spent my days working myself to
exhaustion, my nights half-fearing another Blitz...and death; half-
yearning for it to end the fear."

For an instant, I was afraid she was going to slip back into the
tunnels. She'd begun to pull her knees up to her chest, as she so

often did when reliving the blitz. The nurses would find her huddled in the corner of the room, arms squeezing her knees so tightly that her shoulders and hips would ache for days after. I gave a silent sigh when she straightened her legs and continued the tale.

"I met Charlie in forty-four. He'd lied his way into the army and worked his way up the ranks from Clerk to Supply Sergeant. He wanted to fight, but they'd deemed him unfit for battle. Instead, he was stationed in London."

"Charlie pursued me relentlessly. It took him months to wear me down. Sometimes I wonder if I didn't marry him as much to escape the fear as for love, but marry him I did. He whisked me away to Canada, left me on the family farm and went back to the war. I had no fear of losing Charlie the way I had Andrew, unless the Nazis won the war. If that happened, no one was safe."

It was easy to forget the terror and pain most of the residents had survived. Once a year, the country remembered the sacrifices of the veterans, but I wondered how many ever really considered those who'd been left behind. How many thought about the wars for the rest of the year?

"I worked harder than I thought myself capable of, on that farm. When I had time and energy remaining, I would read Andrews letters. Charlie never wrote. I read them so much, the paper started to wear, and the ink began to fade. I couldn't bear for his words to be lost, so I took a new typing job and saved for a typewriter of my own. It took me forever to type all the letters up, but I finished them before Charlie came home for good."

"So he lives on for you in his words," I mused. The romance of it was touching, even if it was fictional. Daisy really should have tried to publish her story as a novel.

"He lives on still, dearie, but not just in words. He'd never been killed in the war; he'd been captured. Andrew had suffered in a P.O.W. camp in Poland for most of the war; Stalag Luft Three. He wasn't part of the 'Great Escape', mind you." The tears were free now, slipping silently along her cheeks. They followed the lines and folds eighty-four years of living had etched and molded, flouting Newton's laws.

"He'd suffered horribly. Poor, poor, Andrew. He was never quite the same after the war. He was still my Andrew, but quieter...more ethereal."

I wanted to ask how she knew, but I was afraid of breaking the spell she seemed to be under. I still hadn't decided whether she was telling me memories or fantasies, but this was the most coherent, the most spirited, I'd ever seen her. I was prepared to listen to her story as long as she'd tell it.

"He went looking for me, you know, after the war. It was Mother who told him I'd married Charlie and moved to Canada. She said he'd stood still as a stone, silently crying an ocean. After, he'd simply turned and limped away. When I read Mother's letter, I thought I'd die of a bleeding heart. It was two more years before I saw him again. By then, he'd started a completely new life, but he'd brought that life to the nearest town, in Canada."

"Charlie had taken Baby Johnny out to the fields, for the first time, when Andrew came to the house. Andrew had come to introduce himself to the community." There was another long pause as she seemed to lose herself for a second. "We were still desperately in love—we knew it as soon as we saw each other— but I had Charlie and little Johnny, and he had Alice and their new baby, Linda. It broke my heart to see them every Sunday in church. I was never very religious. Andrew hadn't been either…before the camp…." Daisy seemed to collapse into herself.

Lying back, she closed her eyes and tucked her chin into her breastbone. The posture was familiar to me. Daisy was battling with her darker self. I braced myself. That pose usually heralded flying things. Daisy loved to throw things at my head when she was in a "spell". Distracted, I nearly missed her next words. They were softly spoken, and I had to strain to catch them.

"We'd never stopped loving each other. Neither of us would ever want to hurt Alice or Charlie. We loved them in our ways, but we couldn't deny each other. He'd only moved nearby because Mother had told him where I'd gone. He should never have tempted us that way, but I was glad he did. Maybe we'll both go to hell for it, but at least we'll be together."

"Oh, Daisy!" I tried to sound cheerful, despite my shock and disapproval. Really, who was I to judge? Daisy Patterson had lived a long, hard life. I'd never have guessed her an adulteress. Then again, for all I knew, this really was just a story her dementia had twisted into a memory. It wasn't as though anyone could be hurt by it, now. Charlie was certainly past caring. "I'm sure you can be forgiven one little indiscretion" I assured her.

"Fifty-five years tomorrow." She corrected me, wryly. "He's come to me as often as he could. I've loved both of my soldiers nearly all my life…."

I fought down a sigh of relief as she sagged back into the pillows and into sleep. It was all a bitter-sweet fantasy. No one had come to see Daisy in years. She'd been far beyond carrying on an affair as long as I'd known her. I watched her sleep, a sad half-smile playing around her mouth, before checking my watch. It was time to go home; my husband would be hoping for dinner soon.

Her voice startled me as I reached for the door handle. "Take the letters." She said. "Read them for yourself. Perhaps, when I'm gone, you can keep them safe for me."

A thought occurred to me, as I opened my mouth to protest; if I took the aging pages with me, I could read the entire story as I re-typed it into my computer at home. Printed up neatly, I could have it bound as a gift for her birthday in eight weeks. It shouldn't take me more than a month and it would preserve her memories for the rest of her life. Daisy's doctors swore she'd live forever, despite her frail appearance. She'd have years, yet, to treasure those letters. I gathered up the stack of yellowed paper and left.

As I reached the end of the hall, I heard Daisy call out, "I knew you'd come to me today!" I turned to see the tails of a long trench-coat slip through the doorway, as her old pastor limped into her room. With his skeletal, stooped body and deeply etched face, he could have been mistaken for another resident. Only the coat and his trademark fedora separated him from the others. He was obviously very dedicated to his calling; keeping to it long after his retirement.

Daisy passed away in her sleep, her pastor at her side, a few days short of her 85th birthday. I brought her new leather-bound book of letters—her name stamped in gold on the cover—to the group wake. The nursing home held one bi-monthly, for those residents who had slipped away from their tired bodies in the interim.

These events were always uncomfortable for me. Sometimes, the families were tearful, sometimes relieved, often weighed down with guilt. The surviving residents were quietly morose. After the standard prayers and hymns, I spotted Daisy's Pastor, Reverend Simpson, limping toward me purposefully, his fedora cocked jauntily to one side. He stopped before me, stretched his stooped back to stand taller and looked at me sadly. He must have been quite lanky in his youth.

"I believe you have something for me?" he said quietly, the crushing grief obvious through the mask of forced tranquility. Then he smiled with a touch of mischief and offered a slow, broad wink with one bottle-glass green eye, the blue flecks glinting with unshed tears.

How could I not give him the book?

Living Dead

This piece was written as a lyrical poem. Oddly, I was long past the bitterness of the events serving as my inspiration. Perhaps, that is what allowed me the clarity to write about it.

Lying wide awake and wracked with pain,

in bonds too tight to draw the breath to scream.

I could drag you down to witness if I tried,

but I'd rather bind it in the shreds of pride

And my spirit was merely a token.

It shattered long before I fell,

but my soul was never meant to be opened,

and you consigned it straight to hell,

within my head.

Just a foot apart the gulf's too vast,

to save us from delusions of the past

and illusions that deny a fractured home,

when beside you I am never more alone.

Never thought I'd be taken for granted.

You gave away what I won't sell.

If you want to reap the harvest you planted,

you know you'll find it in the hell

within this bed.

And my spirit was merely a token.

It shattered long before I fell.

But my soul was never meant to be opened

and you consigned it straight to hell.

I'm living dead.

No Cookies Today

> *"No Cookies Today" was a free-write*
> *short story. Every Thursday at "The Writers*
> *Block" the lovely Nai'lah Carter presents*
> *her fellow wordsmiths with a "muse". For*
> *twelve hours, writers respond with a piece*
> *inspired by the muse, via twitter at*
> *#DropALine, or on her web page. This story*
> *was my contribution for Session 13.*
> *The muse? "When I saw the joy in that*
> *kid's eye…"*

The lineup at the grocery store cash-out was a mile long at least. Didn't that just figure? My hubby's "to do" list for the weekend was probably twice as long as the line, and I'd already been gone two hours on my "quick" run for groceries. The kiddies would have been up from their naps for an hour, at least, by now. If I was lucky, I wouldn't find him on the front porch, curled in fetal position with a bald spot from pulling his hair out. To say my own nerves were frazzled, would be an understatement.

I swear I'd hit every red light today. Two of the stores I needed to get to were closed. My favorite butcher shop had, apparently, gone bankrupt. I was *not* happy to be stuck in line at the discount grocery store, my arms shaking from the weight of the basket I'd loaded up. I should have grabbed a cart, damn it! Making matters worse, the woman in line, just in front of me, had one child trying to climb the magazine display and a baby in the cart throwing a temper tantrum. My head was going to burst; I just knew it.

I have to give the single, beleaguered cashier credit. She kept the line moving quickly, even managing some friendly chatter with the customers. As her hands scanned barcodes and keyed in coupon codes, with the efficiency of an automaton, she managed to make the standard pleasantries sound positively sincere.

The women with the two mini-demons finally made it to the end of the conveyor belt. She unloaded her groceries slowly, looking as though it took all her energy to do so. Every item hovered above the black strip for a moment, as though she were carefully considering each selection. Formula and baby food went first, then dairy, fruits and vegetables; meats were last. There were no impulse items in her cart. No ice cream, chocolate or dessert items, and not one can of cola.

I looked down at my basket guiltily; the package of cookies, two bag of chips, and two large bottles of ginger ale suddenly looking extravagant and unnecessary. The older monster in front of me must have followed my gaze.

"Cookies, Mommy! Can we have cookies?" I'm sure people in the parking lot could hear him.

"No, honey; no cookies today," the mother shushed him, her face turning an indescribable shade of pink. She turned to focus on the L.E.D. display above the cash register, ignoring the resulting tantrum more effectively than anyone else in the store.

When the cashier told her the total, all the color was sucked out of her face in a blink, and back again just as quickly, but darker. She leaned over and spoke softly to the cashier, who discreetly removed three pounds of hamburger from the bagging area, making a few quick keystrokes on her machine. The woman swiped her debit card, staring nervously at the keypad until a single beep sounded. She sighed deeply, moving her cart around to bag her purchases.

The three pounds of ground beef were stacked precariously on the edge of the register as the cashier reached for the in-house phone. With a quick wave of my hand, I caught her attention, reached over and pulled the packages onto the belt with my own purchases. I paid cash to save time and managed to catch the small family at the front door. Without a word between us, I put the three pounds of ground beef, the package of cookies, and one bottle of ginger-ale into her cart. The mother nodded her thanks solemnly, but it was the boy who brought me to tears. The look of joy in that kid's eye, when he saw those cookies go in the cart, made me think of my own babies at home.

I cried all the way back. My two kiddies greeted me at the door like I'd been gone a year.

"Did you get any cookies, Mama?" my daughter asked immediately, her baby brother waiting for my answer eagerly.

"No, honey; no cookies today." I echoed softly. I pulled them both into my arms for a hug, looking up at my husband with tears still in my eyes. He just nodded, somehow understanding. He knows me well.

Possess

What happens when you find your soul mate? I'm blessed enough to be able to answer that question, at least for myself.

You possess me

Haunt my dreams

Embrace my soul

I have shared with you

Everything I am

Risked for you

Everything I have

Given you

All I might become

Entrusting you

With the means to protect

Or destroy me

With a thought and a breath

You could use my own voice

To break me

To strip me of all that I have

Leaving me

Bereft

And even then

I confess

I would bind to you

The fragments

The Unscheduled Stops

Of my heart and soul

Only you

For one hundred lives

Each one

To possess me

Thief's Moon

> *A bit of a take-off from my usual writing, this erotic story was a challenge, and written in response to a challenge. I attempted something steamy, but romantic as well.*

YOU ~ You were deep in dreamless sleep, when something roused you; a sound in the room, beneath the click and whirr of the fan you'd put on to circulate the stifling, summer night air. A whisper of cloth against cloth. Your mind lurched, brushing at the cobwebs of sleep. You'd left the French doors open to the balcony. Surely no one got in that way. An animal, perhaps? You reached for the lamp as the night sky lit up, immediately before a deafening crack of thunder. Ah, a storm! It must have rolled in while you were sleeping. Not bothering with the lights, you strolled out to the kitchen for a glass of water.

Passing back through the dining room, water in hand, you checked the storm through the balcony doors. The rain was light. None of it was blowing in. You opened the door wider to let in more of the cooling air. A ripple of stray electricity danced over your skin with the next lightning strike. You would have loved to stay up and watch the storm, but your body was begging for sleep.

You slipped back into the bed. The sheets had cooled, sliding over your feverish skin, a silken wave of respite. It took a few minutes, but soon you were sliding back into sleep. You felt that drop—as if the mattress suddenly collapsed two inches beneath you—which sometimes comes just before you lose awareness.

Something brushed your arm…a mosquito? You flicked at it, annoyed. It returned; the whisper of a wing against your cheek. It took a moment to register that you hadn't heard any buzzing.

Your eyes flew open. A familiar face hovered above you, barely visible in the dim light. She was smiling at first, and then she looked surprised, nervous, even a little frightened. Were you dreaming, still? You could see no more than a face and a spill of hair. As the fan swung around, it caught a lock of hair, blowing it toward you. It skimmed your chin. You reached out carefully, depth perception disrupted by the darkness and your own drowsy state. When the tips of your fingers brushed her lips, an electric shock arched between them. She smiled again and closed her eyes; joy and desire on her face. She sighed your name, moving to kiss you very, very softly. Again, she whispered your name against your lips, and "I love you" into your mouth as it opened. You felt her body meld to your side as she covered your mouth again, before you could speak, and her hair fell around your face; a curtain against the night.

You wanted to ask how she got here—how she got in—but the heat, surging electricity and passion, had smothered your voice. You surrendered to it and slipped your arms around her shoulders, rolling to meet her. Lightning illuminated the room as her breath quickened. She was wearing some kind of black bodysuit; Lycra, or spandex. It was molded to her, an illusory second skin. As the echoing glare faded from your vision, her body became invisible again, only real where you touched.

ME ~ It wasn't easy getting onto your balcony, but the yearning in me had given me ingenuity and strength to accompany determination. I'd crouched for half an hour in the shadows, catching my breath; not easy with my heart pounding. The black wool balaclava I'd worn, to hide my face and hair, felt strangely restrictive tonight, but I couldn't remove them. After all, getting arrested for climbing onto your balcony was not what I was trying to accomplish. I'd eluded the law easily enough these past five years. The burglaries were so much easier. There was nothing personal in them. I was in complete control when I worked.

Perhaps that was why I'd chosen that life; why I turned away from you. I was never in control with you. You didn't even have to touch me to have me surrender completely. You were the only thing I ever feared, yet I fell in love with you. I couldn't play by the rules like everyone else. How did I fall in love with someone sworn to uphold them?

It wasn't so bad when you'd been a defense lawyer. At least then we were standing on the same side of the courtroom. You'd been a passionate advocate for my father. It didn't hurt that he was innocent, I suppose. I didn't bother to hide what I was from you. When you switched sides, taking the higher-paying prosecutor's position, I left. I couldn't ask you to risk your career for me, but I wasn't ready to give up mine, either.

I finished my last job a week ago. It was close; the closest I've ever come to getting caught. The rewards were no longer worth the risk. They were never worth what I'd sacrificed. It took me five years to realize it, but I knew it wasn't too late. I'd been watching. Sometimes, I wondered if you never moved into a higher security building because you knew I would. Not that it would matter; there wasn't a security system I didn't know how to bypass. It was the old woman letting her dog out for a piddle, or the half-drunk neighbour stumbling home at three in the morning who were the greater danger.

I'd planned to come tonight. It was the new moon—the thief's moon—and the night was at its darkest. Tomorrow would begin the Celtic Moon of Claiming. I hadn't planned for the storm, though I felt it coming all day; the energy building, feeding the hunger in me; the want. By noon, the want had become undeniable need.

I left my black sneakers in the darkest corner of the balcony, and crept through your apartment with agonizing slowness. The thunder was beginning to rumble in the distance, each low growl increasing my excitement. I could feel the power gathering as I crawled toward the empty side of the bed. Another rumble of thunder. You stirred. The sudden fear, excitement and anticipation were like an injection of some energized aphrodisiac. The rush better, by far, than any carefully planned heist. My body was humming and shivering in reaction.

When the lightning struck, I instinctively pressed myself to the floor and the side of the bed. I needed you vulnerable, unable to protest until it was too late. If I allowed you time to think, all my efforts might be for naught. I would not be denied. I'd waited too long.

Watching you leave the room—your silhouette as the lightning flashed again—a knife of longing sliced through me. I caught my breath when you returned, throttled down the urge to leap at you. I made myself wait. When your breathing was even again, I finally relieved myself of the balaclava.

I stood and watched you for a minute, drinking in the milky shimmer of moonlight spilling across your broad chest and down. The light tumbled over the rippled flesh below your ribs, the flow narrowing until it disappeared, too soon, near your waist. I saw a feast to be devoured; an alter upon which to worship. As the air from the fan cooled my face, the fires inside me raged. The lightning, at rest outside, flashed through my veins, as though I'd taken it into myself instead. I timed your breathing, slipping carefully into the bed, hoping the deep inhale would conceal my entrance. I'd intended to seduce you out of sleep, using my hands and mouth to arouse you; dragging you out of sleep and into me. Unprepared for the effect your placid face would have on my heart, I was immobilized by the sight. Even when you flicked your hand at me, I couldn't move. I no longer needed to just have you; I craved you, body and soul. It hadn't been in the plan to wake you gently. I had no idea I thought to kiss you until I nearly had. When you're eyes flickered open, I panicked for a moment. Would you know it was me, or lash out instinctively? Would you cry out? Would you kick me out?

Your eyes were hazy and full of wonder. You reached, your fingers touching my lips sending a lightning bolt through my veins, suspending reason. Your name escaped me with a sigh. I had to kiss you. You opened your mouth as I drew away, perhaps to protest. I whispered love, pressed myself against you and kissed you again; both in the attempt to stop you and to appease the overpowering need to feel your lips again; to pull your body against mine. You responded and slipped your arms around me and drew me close. The lightning flashed again, and I was electrified.

I wanted to touch you everywhere at once, with hands and lips, but I was no longer in control. My breath coming fast, I threw my head back, arched against you, reveled in the heat of our bodies and raged against the barrier of clothes. Your hands began to caress me, sliding over the slick fabric of the bodysuit, leaving trails of fire. My own hands traveled quickly, randomly over your skin, remembering the curve of each muscle as it tightened in reaction. Your lips found my throat, tearing a moan from me. My hands flew to your head, raking into your hair, pulling you closer until your teeth grazed the skin. You growled low, the vibrations shooting into my flesh as you nipped my throat. I was an inferno. Arching, squealing, I threw my head back farther, exposing more of my neck. It was an instinctive gesture of surrender. Pressing myself into your hips, I willed my body to become an extension of yours; pleading.

You pulled back and smiled, looking into my eyes as they flew open, shocked at the abrupt halt. You drew a breath to speak.

I couldn't allow it. I couldn't chance that you'd try to stop me. I bit your shoulder as I slid a hand between us to stroke your sex. You were hard and pulsing already. The lightning flashed again, outside and through me, ripping a cry from my throat. Your hands fell away from me and, like a hunting cheetah, I struck. I threw my leg over your chest, spinning and diving to take you into my mouth with a feral growl. Your body stiffened in reaction. To what? I didn't care. All that mattered was the smooth, hot, sweet length of you against my tongue. All I knew was the throb and swell as I slowly drew back, the blood roaring in my head, and the aching in my center. I heard you gasp, then moan, and I responded, sending the vibrations through you.

You lurched up under me, grabbing my thighs to pull me to your mouth. You nipped at the fabric. I released you with a primal howl of frustrated need. I squirmed and fought, but your grip was too strong. In complete control now, you nuzzled and bit. You didn't relent when I started to whimper and thrash, instead becoming more intent, and fierce. I tried to cry a warning, but all I could manage was a strangled scream, as release came with the next stroke of lightning.

Freed from your grip, I could do no more than roll to the side, collapse, and gasp for breath. Standing, you flipped on the light, and returned to lie nose to nose with me. I looked into your eyes, losing my soul in the warm, penetrating depths of them. Without a word, you searched my face for whatever answers you needed. I knew the instant you found them.

A glimmer of moisture formed, your pupils expanded. You kissed me deeply with quiet passion, and tenderly helped me undress.

Both naked, we explored with lips and tongues. We relearned each other's bodies, delicately, reverently. I drew faint lines with my fingertips, barely touching your skin, eyes closed, memorizing. I listened for every gasp, hiss and moan that would remind me where your pleasure zones were hidden. You skimmed and kneaded, teased and kissed. Everywhere you touched, I tingled and smoldered. With my savage urgency temporarily appeased, you were indulging our emotions, as much as desire. When my own searching hand found you still eager, I opened my eyes. I slithered out from under your hands to lie level with your hips. My hand gripped you, low, tugging you gently toward me. The smooth, swollen tip fascinated; the glistening of salted sweetness beckoned. I flicked out the tip of my tongue to capture a forming pearl, savouring before I bathed you with my swirling tongue. I wet my lips, kissed the crown, and then opened my mouth slightly to inhale you. As I languidly took you in, my tongue danced, exploring, moaning at every responding pulse. I kept my lips soft and pliant, the only pressure from my tongue, to draw out more of your sweetness. I was utterly absorbed, memorizing with my mouth as I slid my lips back down, and up again. I heard your breathing speed up, challenging me. I moaned again and moved faster. You were burgeoning as the frenzy returned. A flash of brilliant light, with the crash and roll of thunder, spurred our urgency. I growled, kneaded, and moaned. Your hands found my hair, tangled in the length of it, as you began to buck in response. I throbbed and clenched in shared rapture, bolts of electricity racing from my mouth to my center, and back again. I was wet, aching and hungry, but I wanted this to be for you, for all the times I'd denied us both. I didn't stop when you bucked and cried out. I fought to control my animal savagery, the fierce demand, my vicious thirst for you. I rode the peak, euphoric to be with you, giving such pleasure.

I slid up the bed to look into your eyes, again. I loved the loss of control, of self; the complete trust I could have in you, to envelope me, lay me bare, and hold my heart, without the fear of never resurfacing. It had taken a long time to get over that fear and embrace your intense, emotional power, in the past. I gloried in it now, finally free to do so openly. You pulled me to you, my length fitting against yours, as always, like we'd been two halves of a whole all along. Rolling me onto my back, you covered my body with yours and lowered your head to kiss me.

The kiss was long and lingering. Our lips and tongues ever-probing, teasing, urging each other to higher passion, and hotter fever. I felt you surge against my belly and opened myself to you. Lightning flashed, thunder boomed; you broke the kiss when I whimpered. I cried out when you lifted your head, opening eyes and mouth to beg you not to stop. The words died in my throat as my eyes met yours. They were full of questions, but you asked only one, in a voice full of restrained need, "Mine?"

"Yours." I whispered back, my eyes filling with tears, "Now. Always. Only yours." Outside, the skies opened up and the rain poured down. Inside, another storm raged.

Desire

In the midst of writing "Learn to Love Me" I joined a Facebook group for artist and writers. "Volley View", a true online community, is an oasis of talented people, Some of those members are writers of dark romance and the supernatural. This piece was inspired by them.

Surrendered throat

from which you feed,

offering eternity.

The moon's soft sigh

brings the tide.

Desire, consuming me.

Thunder rumbling,

the lightening freed,

crackling electricity.

A hurricane

bringing rain.

Desire, consuming me.

Sacrifice made,

the storm recedes,

just as destiny decreed.

In blood I drowned,

soul unbound.

Desire consuming me.

Chance

This was another piece written for "The Writers Block"/#DropALine, (refer to the author's note for "No Cookies Today"). The muse for Session 14 was, "F**k It!"

Someone was watching me. Of course, in the crowded club, it was quite possible several people were watching me at one point or another. This was different, though. The sensation began as a brush across my consciousness. My breath hitched, and my heart tripped over its rhythm momentarily. The feeling passed as quickly as any glance, in the crush of people gyrating to the pounding music from the band. It was already too late to pinpoint when I scanned the people closest to me. Most of the attention nearby was on the waitress, tapping her foot as she awaited my response to her abrupt "Wha'cha havin'?"

The mind-numbing combination of her peach-on-white, striped balloon skirt with an oversized, lime sweater barely fazed me. More disturbing, by far, was her garishly painted face. Under the multiple layers of foundation hid a beautiful girl, with a rough as sandpaper attitude, and vacant eyes. She'd done an admirable job of hiding the bruises, but she couldn't hide the way she flinched whenever someone near her moved too quickly. I shivered, remembering another young girl who'd dressed to repel, and worn a mask to hide her pain.

"Well?" she prompted.

"Make it a Painkiller. Looks like you could use one, too." She shot me a dirty look as she headed for the next table. I should have known better. She had to decide to help herself. No stranger was going to get through to her until she was ready to listen.

There it was again, a fingertip skimming down my spine and back up to the base of my neck. Gooseflesh rose on my arms, the turtleneck of the sleeveless sweater suddenly too tight around my throat. It wasn't a creepy sensation, more of an uncomfortably sensual tingle. I stared at the tabletop in front of me, ostensibly studying the grain of the wood, but actually tuning in to my peripheral vision. Two men at the table on my right were openly appraising me, while engaged in animated conversation. There was a woman pointing me out to her girlfriend, or rather, pointing out my handbag. I was tempted to walk over and tell her where I'd bought it. A third man leaned against the rail along the left wall, his dark eyes drifting away casually as I lifted my head to look at him, an amused smile playing about his full lips.

"Can I get you a drink?" It was one of the men from the right table. He was overdressed for this place, in a suit less the tie. Three tasteful, gold chains graced his thick neck. His perfectly arranged hair gleamed like plastic in the lights from the dance floor. He stood carefully erect, sucking in his stomach a little, which strained the smile he was trying to hold. I had no patience for insincerity, small minds, or big egos. Besides, something in the way he held himself spoke "bully" to me.

"Thank you, but I just ordered one." He was making an effort to be civil, at least. I could do as much in return.

"Are you waiting for someone?"

"No, but I don't come here for the company. I come to listen to the bands."

"Groupie?" He laughed as he asked, but the laugh was more forced than the smile had been. I didn't bother to respond.

"I'm Nathaniel." The words were rushed, desperate sounding. He held out a hand for me to shake.

I felt it again. Eyes focused on me with an intensity that made me shiver; an invisible hand caressing my face. I fought the sensation.

"Would you like to join my friend and me, …? " He was hoping for a name. I wasn't about to offer one.

"Well hello, Love." A hand settled on my left shoulder; the thumb stroking lightly. I did my best not to jump. "I didn't expect you to be here tonight." The electric heat radiating through the sweater was a pleasant surprise. Nathaniel pulled himself up even taller, flexing his chest a little, as he stared with obvious disdain over my shoulder at the interloper. I bit back a laugh.

"Just play along." He whispered in my right ear. The urge to giggle wafted away. His voice was deep, smooth, with a bit of gravel for added texture. His whisper was all breath and purr. His breath smelled of ginger and sugar. He kissed me softly on the side of my head, his hand slipping down my arm. My heart threw itself against my ribs.

Nathaniel shrank three full inches in height, flushed and slumped back to his table. The hand slipped off my elbow as the man behind took the chair on my left, allowing me to turn my back on my erstwhile suitor, and his companion.

His eyes were gorgeous! Burnt honey and melted chocolate; they were earthy, warm, and sparkling with mischief. I was drawn into them even as I tried to pull away. He had little laugh lines at the corners, not deep enough to be called crow's feet. His lips were drawn into the same amused smile I'd seen as he'd leaned against the rail. I wanted to kiss them and slap him, at the same time.

"I didn't need the help." I hissed, throwing indignation up as a shield. "I'm a big girl. I can handle one boy all by myself."

"Undoubtedly! But wasn't this easier?" He stared into my eyes, neatly side-stepping the verbal thrust.

"Run!" my brain screamed. "Hide!" my heart warned. The last thing I needed right now was another man to deal with. I'd had enough of being manipulated and controlled by pick-up artists, and con-artists. It may have been a lonely six months, but at least I'd had no one to please but myself. No longer did I feel the need to have a man "take care of me". I was stronger than I'd ever been.

The waitress returned, plopping my drink down in front of me. She turned to the man beside me, eyes softening with sisterly affection. "Hey, John! Another ginger-ale?"

"Hey, Cindy! You give that idiot the boot?" It was less a question than a statement.

"Yeah." She grimaced. "Thanks for the reference. The new place is nice."

"No problem. You can do better, kid...I'll have one more."

The short exchange was illuminating. There was a kind heart behind the mischievous smile. Here was a man intelligent and compassionate enough, to help the girl help herself. I could feel my defenses thinning. I couldn't deny the attraction to this stranger, who somehow seemed so familiar.

John turned his attention back to me. How did he make me feel like the only woman in the universe? The rest of the bar faded. It was almost like everything around us had gone slightly out of focus. The music even sounded muffled, like it was being played in a separate room. I glanced suspiciously at my drink, but I hadn't touched it yet.

I tried shaking my head, to rid it of the fog. NO! This was not some fairy tale. There was no way I was going to allow myself to be sucked in by a handsome face, gorgeous eyes, kissable lips, talented hands…aw, fuck it! Who the hell was I trying to fool? I could stay locked inside myself, or I could take a chance.

The world returned for a second with Cindy. She set John's drink on the table, with a wink at him, and an encouraging smile for me. As Cindy turned away, John turned those amazing eyes back to me, again. They widened in delighted surprise, to find me so close. I held my breath, closed my eyes, and kissed him. When he kissed me back, I knew I was doomed.

Landlocked

> *An experiment in poetry, from a character perspective, with emphasis on metaphors.*

The lights on the water flicker an invitation.

The voice of the waves calls me to the deep.

The taste of sea-spray lingers with temptation.

Within my grasp, escape is sadly sweet.

Myriad memories distort the vision,

and unnamed fears drown out the sea's sweet call.

My heart cries out in sudden indecision,

But freedom's siren strengthens my resolve.

Don't call my name for my heart won't here you.

Don't try to stop me. It's too late

to change my mind. I've waited too long.

This time I will not hesitate.

I stride toward the waves with all conviction,

that my fate lies far beyond this dismal shore.

Too much, by far, I feel the land's restriction.

The sea will be my home forevermore.

A Startling Character

> *This story was my entry into the "Bo's Café Life Fiction Contest". The subject: Café Life. The limit: 1000 words.*

I had everything I needed; notepad, pencils, erasers, keen eyes and an active imagination. This writing assignment would be fun, I thought. The directions were simple; observe a stranger, in a public place and write a short story about them. The cafe was the perfect place. As often as I avoided the other customers while writing, I enjoyed the conversation I was sometimes drawn into. The place was usually full of characters waiting to be discovered or created.

I found a seat with the best view of the whole cafe. Sipping at my scalding-hot cup of black gold, I scanned the patrons. I saw him immediately...

It wasn't the young guy in the corner, rocking out to the music, fully audible despite the ear-buds, as he read a textbook of some sort..."Rise Against," if I heard correctly. Not the poor sap with the hairnet, behind the counter, looking miserable. I wasn't more than contemptuously amused by the young, Romeo biker, and his harem of twittering, teen girls. No, my character was new to the café. He sat quiet, alone in the corner, clinging to his steaming mug with craggy hands, muttering to himself.

What was it that had captured my interest? Was it his stillness? Only his full, dark lips were moving. The rest of his body appeared to be in self-imposed rigor mortis, leaning forward and staring intently at the window, as though some invisible companion sat across from him, engaged in quiet debate. No, my eyes should have skipped right over him; an inert bit of decoration. It was his eyes. Not the flickering, mad-burn of reflected lights within. His eyebrows had drawn my attention. The left was brown-black like his hair, and quite small and neat. The right like a pair of wild rosebushes in winter; shrouded in frost and split by a bare space in the exact centre. A dark, circular scar marred the exposed skin. Each long, scraggly hair was bright white.

He couldn't have been more than forty, the olive skin of his face barely lined, with the exception of one etched deep across his forehead. What had caused the odd eyebrow and scar? Why did he talk to himself? Why did his hands look so old? Where had he come from? Did he live in his own reality?

The waitress passing his table tripped over nothing; the full mug on her tray flying toward the studying rocker. My subject put himself between the scalding liquid and its oblivious victim, in the space of half a breath. One hand caught the spinning mug, the other prevented the waitress' fall. He didn't blink when the coffee splattered his jacket. The girl was frantically apologizing, and dabbing at his shirt, before she'd regained her balance.

I wasn't gawking at him alone, now. A couple, several tables over, watched in stunned silence. The bevy of teens giggled nervously, staring. When he finally moved again, it was to stoically remove the jacket, and return to his seat. Other than the waitress, now mopping at the mess on the floor, everyone in the café was gaping at the impossibly quick stranger with one bushy, white brow.

He raised his head deliberately, and scanned the room. My mind was spinning, trying to encompass this man and turn him into a viable character. His eyes met mine, dark cappuccino, radiating emotion I couldn't fathom. Light flashed in them as he broke the gaze, like lightning…lightning…lightning-fast.

Crackling air and the smell of the rain. I felt the gathering electricity dance across my skin. A banshee screech, a blinding flash of light and exquisite pain. A woman's voice, "Devon!"

That was it, Devon! He'd been struck by lightning, just above the eye. No. It sounded so cliché, but something about it just fit! Had it damaged his brain? Had it brought the tensed posture and mumbling? Still in a surreal state, I watched him lazily make eye contact with some of the others. As if his stare released them from some spell, they averted their eyes, suddenly anxious to resume whatever they'd suspended. What did he see? What would I see through his eyes?

"The couple, first. The girl's nervous. She's been tearing her napkin to bits, making a nest of them. Symbolic? Maybe. The nest she hopes to make with the boyfriend. Only one she's getting, and she knows it. More perceptive than she knows, that girl. He doesn't want to play house, he just wants to play. Time to move on, Ashley; he has no intention of settling down."

"Do you, Brad? Brought her here to end this, didn't you? She's not the type to make a public scene. Better hurry. That new dolly's a hottie, but she won't stand for being stood up. She'll teach you a thing or two, just not what you're hoping. Be nice, now. You'll break her heart, but there's no call to be cruel."

"Well now, Mr. Music-man. Ace is it? Ah, Tracey. Don't like the name your mother gave you? Better turn down that noise and crack those books. You've got a tough haul to pass. Don't bother asking Stacey out, son. Our little waitress is engaged. Just doesn't wear the ring here."

"Smart girl, Stacey: better tips for a pretty, single girl. Perceptive lads would see that tan-line, but most aren't looking at your hands, now are they? You could do up a button or two and still cash in."

I was thoroughly enjoying my fanciful dialogue; so much, I didn't feel his gaze return.

"Ah, the wanna-be novelist. If you really want to succeed girl, better find your own words and stop stealing mine."

My heart stopped as I read what I'd written! When I lifted my head, he was staring at me, the corner of his lips twitching and humour glittering in his eyes. He gave me a slow wink.

Carmaterdea

Carmaterdea was originally crafted for the charity anthology, "Rise of the Goddess: Divine Awakenings." Each contributor wrote a short story about a fictional or mythological goddess.

The original purpose of the anthology was to raise money for a small library, in Omaha, in danger of losing its children's programs.

Carmaterdea surveyed her new neighbourhood with cautious optimism. It was a fixer-upper, alright. The open pathways on the outer fringes were nice enough, but the farther she moved toward the well-lit center, the more drifting litter she saw. The first few places in the neighbourhood looked cold and uninviting. Those closest to the centre were too garishly bright. The third one back from the middle, though, that was more promising. The blues, greens and rich browns were soothing to her mind's eye. If Carm could clean up the trash around it, do something about any infestations, and scrub it up a bit, it might just suit her needs. The first thing to do was get rid of the trash keeping her from taking a closer look. With one great sweep, she brushed aside a few billion dollars' worth of technology.

~When every satellite crashed at once, the general population stared at their blank screens, or shouted obscenities at the air. The great powers on Earth looked to the heavens and cried out in fear. ~

That was much better. Now Carm could get a clear look at the inhabitants. Since the majority of this ball was water, she checked in the centre of the largest ocean first. The diversity was impressive! Someone had done a great deal of work here to produce such a variety of life. The creatures were all shapes and sizes, all colours and patterns. Most of them were very quiet. A few were more boisterous. The most impressive, by far, were the largest. They, Carm decided, must be chief among the creatures.

> ~They sang to each other in voices full of tenderness and melancholy. A great mother nuzzled her baby and crooned to him softly. ~

The sound lulled her senses for a moment, until one of the younger voices rose in panic. She scanned for its source.

Oh, the folly! An island of unnatural filth marred the beauty of this ocean, some of it floating on the surface and more snaking through the water all the way down to the ocean bed. More garbage cluttered the surface, closer to the shores of great masses of land. Among the litter, a metal machine cut through the water. She watched in horror as tiny, bipedal animals scurried around the object, shouting to each other in harsh strings of sound.

Tiny Deuses! Dammit! Carm thought she'd left all divinities behind.

A large arrow launched away from the machine and impaled the great mother, even as it tried to escape. Where was the creator of this world? Why wasn't it here to stop this atrocity? What *were* these horrible miniature Deuses?

Carm extended her will. She removed the sharp device from the body of the gentle creature, and healed the wounded flesh. She created a giant wave and sent it after the death machine.

~The men screamed, throwing their hands up at the face of the wave, as though they could somehow fend it off. One clung to the rail and sent up a fervent prayer. Another sketched a sign against evil into the air, even as he slid into the angry water. ~

The machine roared toward the nearest Island. The land was cluttered with even more garbage, and so many vermin that she could barely see the soil for their constructions. The wave grew with her fury. She would have it cleanse the land.

"Stop!" The voice of a Deus cried out from behind her perception. "This is *mine*. You have no right to meddle with my work."

It had been too much to hope that this planet had been abandoned. The whole point of her relocation was to put a galaxy or two between Carm and her kin.

"Your work is doing a fine job of ruining itself. I was just fixing things," she projected into the void of space. She wouldn't give him the satisfaction of looking for him. Let him come to her. "You should be thanking me. These vermin are attacking other creatures, and they're devastating the water and land. How long have you left this planet unattended?"

"You are wrong, Goddess. Those *vermin* are my charges, given the others creatures to sustain them. *You* will ruin everything with your temperamental wave."

If Carm had selected a corporeal form yet, she'd have swallowed some part of it.

It made much more sense, and somehow far less, when the Deus drifted into her focus area, blocking her view of the planet. His features were uncomfortably familiar. His hair was white, with a flowing beard the same, his eyes near-black orbs, and lightning flashed within. He had adopted a form that mimicked them; two arms, two legs, two eyes, and facial hair. This divinity seemed to honour the creatures, yet he made no gesture for their salvation. Was he too weak, this Deus, to counter her?

With a flick of her will, Carm halted the wave and smoothed the waters.

~One of the men cried. Another dropped
to the deck, unconscious. The rest simply
stared at the becalmed sea with wide eyes
and slack jaws. ~

Something was not right here. She would learn more before she intervened further.

"What is your name, Deus?"

"Yes." His eyes had calmed to dark-brown discs, like rich, damp soil, but peppered with specks of starlight.

"You have chosen 'yes' as a name?" He'd gone mad in his solitude, Carm decided.

"Who's on first?" He laughed after he said it, a booming sound.

It only validated her analysis.

> ~People all over the planet looked to the
> sky, wondering at the thunder without
> lightning. ~

"What?" Carm shook her head. He made no sense.

He laughed again, and shook his mighty beard. "A silly human thing. You wouldn't understand. I am known to them by many names, but nearly all of them mean Deus, or God."

"You call them humans, then? An odd—*wait*, you chose Deus as a *name*?"

The corners of his mouth turned up and his eyes flashed. "Aaah! It's been so long since I've had the company of other divinities. There is so much to tell!"

"How can you let them destroy your world? What is your true name? How long have you been here alone?" He seemed harmless enough. A few direct answers would be worth conversation with a rogue God.

"I've nearly forgotten..." He stared at the cloud of cosmic dust that was Carm. "Perhaps you could select a more...traditional form. There is a place where we can rest and speak of things."

"Where?"

"One of our many ancient homes. It's not nearly as pleasant as your domicile, I'm sure, but it was quite beautiful in its day." He moved toward the planet, his diaphanous form becoming more compact and opaque as he drew closer.

Carm couldn't see the harm in following. As the earth drew near, she elected for a feminine version of his corporeal form, though she allowed herself three pair of arms, if only to appease her revulsion of the human creatures.

They came to rest on the highest peak of a mountain. A long cleft in the peak, tilting up on the sides, offered a place for them to sit facing one another. The god waved his arm and clouds gathered beneath, surrounding the mountaintop in a carpet of white, obscuring the two from the world below. Carm could feel the familiar tingle of power she associated with her home on Atlantis.

"What is this place?" She asked.

"This *was* Olympus. When the gods moved the citadel to Atlantis, they took much of the peak with it to form the Island of Atlantis, far from the reach of humankind. Eventually—"

"But Atlantis is not an Island!"

"Perhaps not where it rests now." One corner of his mouth pulled back in a half-grimace and he tilted his head down to look at her from beneath scruffy brows, drawn together.

Carm was in no mood to be chastised by the god. "Well? Go on, then, if you *must* make an epic tale of it!"

He continued to stare for a moment, before picking up his tale. "When the gods grew weary of playing with their human toys—" He stopped speaking to stare at her again. He must have noticed her rolling her eyes, "—they withdrew the citadel to a place across the seas. They lived there quietly for a time, but eventually the humans began to travel farther, and the risk of discovery was too great. It took the combined power of all the Gods to send Atlantis to the part of the universe you know as your home. Some bits remain; the humans call it the Bermuda Islands. To this day, when even belief in gods is rare, superstition lingers around that remnant of our last earthly home."

"So, this is Orbis Terrarum, Gaia Soporatus!" Carm ignored his glare. "Ludum relictus."

"Yes. Earth, the dormant goddess Gaia, and the abandoned game, just as you say. I see my absent kin still cling to much of the human Latin."

"Is it a human language, Latin?"

"Yes. The Gods adopted it." He nodded as he spoke.

"Yet I understand your words, though they are not Latin."

"It's a quality of the gods. We always comprehend one another."

"Who *are* you? You speak of the gods as kin, yet all of them are on Atlantis, aside from Gaia, and —" Something in her memory tickled the back of her tongue. "Prometheus!"

"That was my name once, yes. Now, young goddess, what is yours?"

"Carmaterdea" She stretched the word out slowly to give him the pronunciation. It sounded like Carm-mate-er-dee-ya..

The Gods brows drew together again. "Hmm...karma is an Indian concept. Mater for mother. Dea for goddess. Your mother had great plans for you. Which goddess birthed you?"

She looked to the rock between them. "My mother is Justitia."

"Ah, that explains your indignation, and sense of righteous justice." He nodded, his mouth turning up in a half-smile. "But I asked which *birthed* you."

This god was too clever by far. Carm raised her head and searched his strange eyes. "Vesta." She had the satisfaction of seeing his brows rise, and his mouth fall open.

"The virgin goddess has broken chastity? Now that *is* news!" His expression became inscrutable. "Birthed by Vesta, raised by Justitia." He seemed to be talking to the air, but his gaze returned to her with an intensity that made her assumed skin tingle. "Which god fathered you?"

"None!" She knew, even as she spat the word through clenched teeth, that he would see through her.

"Fine. It's no surprise that many of the gods are horrible fathers. Which conceived you, then?" He asked

Carm fought down anger. She had come here to escape such things. This was to be her new existence, far from the control of the other deities and the animosity of her mother. Gaia, however, intrigued her. She had an overwhelming desire to reclaim and reawaken the most ancient goddess of all. If she left now, she would never find the means to wrest her from the power of Prometheus.

"Saturn. Saturn conceived me on his virgin daughter; an unwanted child, on an unwilling goddess." The words came with anger, no matter how she fought to contain it.

"Ah, youngling! Has he cast you out of Atlantis to assuage his conscience, then?" His voice was soft now, as well as his eyes, but forks of lightning raced through the darkening clouds at their feet. He knew the gods well. Rape was not uncommon amongst them.

"Saturn has no conscience." The venom was palpable. He would ask, she knew: better to just tell him. "I left to prevent war between the goddesses. Vesta would have cast me away at birth, but for Justitia, Venus and Trivia championed Justitia's petition to adopt and raise me to maturity. Vesta has yet to forgive them. Saturn disregarded me until I reached that maturity."

She paused, trying to decide whether to tell him the rest. An earthly hour passed in silence. The god sat, unmoving, and she knew he was waiting for her to finish.

"I left, to keep him from repeating his barbarism." She said.

He reached for her, and she slapped him away. "Do *not* touch me! No god will *ever* touch me!" The cloud carpet began to swirl around the mountaintop, a pseudo-tornado her fury called into being.

"Calm, youngling. I offer comfort, not harm. I am sorry. My brother and his children are—"

"Don't. I want nothing from any Deus, certainly not pity."

"Nothing? Would you condemn me with the others? Me, the one divinity who never abandoned this game? The one who remained behind to protect our many creations?"

She could feel her jaw tensing. "Chiefly the humans. Why?"

"Such difficult questions you ask. I'd forgotten how thirsty the young are for enlightenment." He laughed, and the stone beneath them trembled.

Carm pursed up her lips and rolled her eyes, but she was grateful for the levity. "So, enlighten me."

"We would be here for centuries if I explain it all, child. All the while, the humans are suffering for your curiosity. A moment, if you please?"

The god closed his eyes, and she felt power radiate from him. When he opened them again, he was smiling.

"What have you done?"

"I've restored what you so casually destroyed and cleansed the memory from the minds of the humans. That one swipe of your power created chaos worthy of Eris. The economic structure collapsed, causing riots, looting, murder... It has become a very complex and delicate world. I've left it unmanaged too long, and your ham-handedness did far too much damage to leave it unchecked."

"Why *did* you ignore this world for so long?"

He bowed his head and exhaled heavily. "That too, is part of a greater tale."

"Well, you'd better get started, before eternity runs its course." She laughed, but the sound was hollow.

"It's best to begin at the beginning. You know of Gaia and Uranus?" He waited for her to answer.

She sighed and swallowed her impatience. "How she saved her children and defeated him? Yes, but not what became of him, or how she became dormant."

"Of course, that is glossed over in the legends." He puckered his mouth and stared at the clouds for a moment. "Gaia was rendered dormant by Saturn. Such was her punishment for shielding Jupiter from his murderous intent. He managed it before Jupiter defeated him, just as he had defeated his father before, with Gaia's help. Later, she became the playing field for the Great Game. Now she is simply called Earth."

"And Uranus?"

"Uranus was already dormant and imprisoned within another planet in this solar system. I ensured that when the planet was finally titled, it retained the Latin translation of his original name, though many of the humans resisted my influence, at first."

"And Saturn? How did *he* escape such imprisonment? Why did Jupiter not render him dormant? It would have been just, and saved all of us much grief?"

"I don't know, honestly. If he had, the Great Game may never have come to pass, and the gods would still live on Olympus. I'm sure he regrets it now."

"No. He does not." Carm corrected him. "The gods exist in a constant state of debauchery. Saturn has created a race of slave-creatures for Atlantis. The planet is crawling with them."

His mouth fell open for the second time, but he regained his composure swiftly. "Do they resemble these humans he created?" He asked.

"*Saturn* created the humans? Why?"

"You haven't answered my question. You first, then I will

57

answer."

"No. The Atlantians are colourless, hairless and sexless. The only thing they have in common with humans is their general structure. Each has two arms, two legs and two eyes. They do not eat or drink, but absorb sustenance from the air of the planet. All food and drink are for the Deuses, uh, gods. Atlantians do not breed. Jupiter forms them from clay; Saturn breathes life into them. They exist to serve and provide everything to the Gods. Nothing they do is by their own will or thought."

"Ah, so Saturn *has* learned something!" Prometheus smiled ruefully.

"What do you mean?" Carm was skeptical.

"Despite his carnal weaknesses and general debauchery, which are, sadly, a fundamental element of most divinities, Saturn does— or at least he *did*, attempt to deflect the Olympians from inflicting pain on one another."

"I don't believe you." She said

"What would I gain by a lie?" His voice was calm, but there was a hint of anger in the question.

"If he cared all those millennia ago, he *stopped* caring just centuries back. Now, he is the most abominable of a vile assembly—"

"If I may continue?" He interrupted.

Carm nodded with some reluctance.

"After his defeat by Jupiter, Saturn was banished to the Island of Atlantis, and bound by oath to never challenge the rule of

Jupiter. Truthfully, Saturn was tired of battles by then. He welcomed the solitude. He passed his time making one tiny Island into a ring of islands, connected by ornate bridges and graced with beautiful towers and citadels. He built the citadels by hand, one pink grain of sand at a time, and fused together with the stolen heat of a volcano.

"Come, I will show you where the first Atlantis was."

He led her over Greece, and the Ionian Sea. They skimmed over the Mediterranean. It was only a few minutes before they passed through the Pillars of Hercules, to the vast Atlantic Ocean. As they left Corvo and Flores behind, the god took up his tale again.

"While Saturn thrived in exile, his children, siblings and cousins were at constant war with one another. It was the time of the Gods, alone, and it was chaotic. Saturn could feel the pain, even in his exile. He worried the rest would destroy each other, and Gaia with them. Jupiter worried as well, and he finally sought out his father for advice.

"When Jupiter saw the great crystal towers and citadels of Atlantis, he admired their beauty and function. With Saturn's encouragement, he set the Gods a first task. He demanded they build a citadel atop Olympus. Rather than sand-to-crystal, though, the Olympians chose—"

"White marble. " she interrupted. "Yes, it is the centre of the city on Atlantis now. 'Pro Contione', they call it in Latin, and it's used as a meeting hall.

"Well, it was originally the palace of the Olympians."

"They occupy the towers in the rings of the city now. I cannot imagine the thousands of divinities living in such a small space. "

Prometheus chuckled, and thunder tumbled through the sky. "There were far fewer in those days, though that didn't last long. See, with so many hands to the task, and the large blocks of marble used, the citadel was completed in a trifling. It wasn't long before the gods were at loose ends, and one another's throats, again.

"Ah, here it is! This was where Atlantis stood, before the gods took it to the other end of the universe." He swept an ethereal arm over a bit of green, barely visible, in the great blue water.

Carm peered at a small archipelago atop what appeared to be an underwater mountain.

He gestured to the middle of the archipelago. "This is where they placed the marble citadel. It was the very center of the crystal city and had been a lake until the citadel displaced the water."

"Why did they leave this bit behind?" she asked.

"When they took the crystal city, they found a fault in the bedrock. It was simplest to take everything above the fault and leave the rest, and so they did. In time, the ocean brought sediment and deposited it here. When humans finally discovered the lonely little Island, they would never have guessed it was once a sacred place, but for the aura of strangeness about it. Many myths and superstitions have grown up around this tiny bit of land.

"A century passed and Jupiter sought out Saturn again, begging for assistance in bringing the deities to heel. Together, the two

Gods created the Great Game, a challenge really."

"I heard much whispering about the Great Game, but never in Saturn's presence, and never with detail. What *was* this game?"

"When the gods first came to power, youngling, they were all equal. Despite what the legends tell, none of them had a clearly defined realm of influence, aside from Jupiter's position of leadership. Saturn believed that the bickering and infighting were a direct result of the lack of focus, responsibility, and goals.

There were water, fire, earth and air, but there was also life. It was tiny, nearly imperceptible life, but it existed. With these five tools, the gods and goddesses would create the flora and fauna which now populate this planet. He, or she, who created the most complex and beautiful life form, would control the planet and rule over the other Olympians. Jupiter would retire to Atlantis with his father. First, they had to swear an oath to cease the direct battles between them. The gods embraced the challenge, and all agreed to swear the oath."

Now the diversity of this planet made more sense to Carm. She peered at the clouds, willing them to part, but they did not move.

"Patience. I will show you more when you understand *why* it exists. Perhaps then you will not be so resolute to awaken Gaia, and destroy it all."

Carm flinched. Were her thoughts so transparent?

"Nearly as tangible as my own." He chuckled again. "You are young, and I have more experience with such things.

"The competition was fierce, but the planet was eventually

populated with millions of new species. Some were beautiful in their simplicity, some overwhelmingly complex. At least the deities were no longer trying to destroy one another.

"As the beauty of Earth increased, so did Jupiter's desire to remain in control of it. He returned to Atlantis. With Saturn's assistance, Jupiter worked on his own contribution in secret. Unlike the other creatures the gods created, which were drawn from the imagination and desire, the models for this creature were the Olympians."

"Humans."

"Yes, the humans. A male human, to be exact, though Jupiter didn't breathe life into his man until he'd also fashioned him a female companion, a woman. Even then, he refrained from revealing his masterpieces. He was patient.

"The gods were becoming frustrated with the contest. Each looked at the creations of the others and worried that their creations weren't good enough. They were weary of trying to outdo each other. Some focused on altering their creations, and setting them upon each other. These creatures would devour and destroy their competitors. The deities changed the rules among themselves, coming to an agreement that the creature that defeated all the others would be declared the winner."

"And then Jupiter revealed the humans."

"Not right away. However, with the co-operation of the full pantheon, he put limitations on how the creations could be altered, and he set a deadline for the judging to begin. He convinced the others that Saturn should judge, as the only god not participating in the competition.

"But that isn't fair! Saturn *was* participating. He was helping Jupiter."

"Correct, but the other gods didn't know that. Jupiter went back to Saturn, and they altered his humans. Saturn gave them tremendous potential to learn and evolve on their own. He gave them the capacity to think, plan, design, and implement. Jupiter gave them a digestive design that would allow them to survive on an incredible diversity of sustenance. He designed them to rule over all the other creatures."

"Jupiter waited until the last possible moment. Only *then* did he release his humans into the world, securing his throne on Olympus."

"So he won the contest," Carm said, "but why did the gods leave Earth? Why abandon all their work?"

"Well, as the humans bred and evolved, flaws in their design became apparent. These first humans knew the divine intimately. The Olympians were fascinated with the men and women, and appalled by them. They looked and acted like the gods, with little of the greater power the divinities possessed. Some thrived, while others withered. Some succumbed to the baser qualities with which the gods were imbued."

"The divinities couldn't resist meddling in the lives of the humans, playing with them like living toys, or pets. Often, a god or goddess would find a favourite man or woman to pamper, and another would meddle. The infighting resurfaced, and it was worse than ever. To forestall the battles, Jupiter called all of them to Olympus and decreed limitations to every interaction with the humans."

"Boundaries were drawn for each of them. They were to have control only over certain aspects of the human lives. That was when the divinities were assigned their spheres of influence. The plan achieved peace for a while, but the Gods have never been proficient at keeping within boundaries, or following rules."

He ignored her chuff of caustic laughter, continuing his tale.

"When the first human woman conceived of a god, Jupiter seemed furious at the apparent defiance. When the woman was brought to Olympus, however, she revealed that it was Jupiter himself who had fathered her unborn child. His inability to abide his own laws opened the floodgate. Soon all the divinities were cavorting with humans, and the age of demigods began."

"What is a demigod?"

The God jumped. His eyes were wide as he stared at Carm, as though he'd forgotten she was there.

"Demigods are the children of women fathered by gods, or the children of goddesses fathered by men. They are not immortal, as the Olympians were, nor as powerful, but far more powerful and longer-lived than humans. Demigods were also less devoted than the humans. By this time, the Gods had fashioned a new game. It began that the deity with the most worshipers was the victor, but the human population was growing exploding, and it soon became impossible to keep count. So, the divinities demanded that their humans show fealty with offerings, gifts and sacrifices. The demigods were defiant. They refused to worship their divine parents and began to meddle in the affairs of the humans."

"The humans revered the demigods as prophets and oracles. The sacrifices dwindled, as did the peace among humans. The Olympians were bound by their oath to bring no harm to one another, and by extension, their offspring. However, Saturn swore no such oath. He had sworn only to let Jupiter rule unchallenged."

"At Jupiter's entreaty, Saturn planned to eliminate the demigods and humans."

"But that doesn't make sense. The humans, animals, plants, insects and birds; they are here, still."

"Yes." Prometheus' voice was barely audible, as he mumbled the word into his beard. "My greatest coup, and my most terrible mistake."

"I know this story! You gave the humans fire."

"No. They had discovered fire on their own, centuries before. I was caught when I tried to give them a bit of the *eternal* flame. My mistake was giving them an escape from Saturn's wrath."

"You saved all the humans?"

"No. I saved two former demigods, my son Deucalion and his wife, Pyrrha. When the demigods' defiance became intolerable, Saturn forced Neptune to cleanse the Earth, much the way you attempted to do. Most of the flora would renew itself in time, and the gods and goddesses brought breeding pairs of the best fauna to

Olympus. All the demigods were summoned to the foot of Jupiter to swear fealty. He granted those who did so sanctuary, and a place in the pantheon as full gods. The rest were sent back to Earth, stripped of their divinity, though they retained longevity."

Deucalion and Pyrrha refused to bow to Jupiter. I was proud of them for their defiance and courage, even as I wept for their fated demise." The god hung his head and his shoulders sagged. "Next, the gods and goddesses, old and newly made, knelt to give oath that we would not interfere on behalf of our pet humans. With so many crowded into the citadel, my absence went unnoticed."

"You didn't swear to anything!"

"I did not. Come, I will show you a simple wonder."

He took her back to Greece. She thought, at first, that they were returning to Olympus, but he drew her farther south to another mountain.

"This is Parnassus," he indicated the mountain, "and here," he waved a hand over the southern face of it, "is what the humans have titled 'the Corycian Cave.'"

Carm peered at the hole in the rock face. It was small, to her, but quite large enough for humans. She watched a group of them enter it with varying degrees of reverence and awe. It didn't look like much to her; rather dark and damp, really. There was a stone at the entrance, with something green clinging to it. Inside, the stalactites of the same green dripped murky water onto the earth floor.

"What is so special about this cave?" she asked the god.

"I hid Deucalion and Pyrrha here for forty years. They survived on food and drink I stole from the halls of Olympus. I brought them wood to burn, for warmth, but it ran out before the Earth was dry again. After the years of effort to save them, I couldn't let them die of the cold." He chuckled, a bitter sound.

~The humans in the cave cringed, looking to the ceiling with eyes wide, as the boom echoed through the depths. ~

"Your birth mother caught me stealing a bit of eternal flame from the citadel. Jupiter was furious, but he was too busy keeping order among the other gods to deal with me. He turned my fate over to your foster mother."

"Your coup was worthy of Mercury." She laughed. The sound of it was the roar of wind and wave, and the quaking of the stone. It was the first time she had truly laughed in decades.

~Some of the humans urged the others out of the caves. No few of them were shouting and crying. ~

Prometheus beckoned her away, and they drifted back to Olympus.

"Justitia would not condemn me without knowing the circumstances. It was she who discovered the Deucalion and Pyrrha, and she who passed my eternal judgement. Since I had gone to such lengths to save humankind, I would be responsible for their protection forever."

"But the other gods—"

"Were weary of the Great Game." He finished for her. "They no longer cared for the humans, or their fate. Saturn was furious at being thwarted, and Jupiter at being deceived, but they had given Justitia the decision, and she made her decree. I was to be the last remaining god on Earth." He settled back on the mountaintop again, and she sat across from him.

"But how—"

"Oh, it was easily done. The gods gifted Deucalion and Pyrrha a new set of memories. Mercury rewrote some of our best tales and made them the work of a single deity, rather than a pantheon. Afterward, the deities retired to Atlantis. They took the citadel with them, along with the peak of Olympus. We sit on barely half of the original mountain, as we speak."

"So you are responsible for all of humanity. There were no chains, no great eagle feasting daily on your liver?" Carm felt her mouth quirking as she teased him.

"No, child." There was no laughter from him, now. "They set me a greater torment than that. I was to watch my descendants suffer all manner of torture in life. Even those who do not suffer, but thrive, must wither and die within a century, as I do nothing but observe.

"But why? Why not intervene? Why have you let them come to this?"

"I'm not permitted to do more, nor have I the will remaining. It has been more than two millennia since I have had the consciousness even to watch them." His eyes had turned black once more, and he stared at her feet. Pain radiated from him, with force enough to render her immobile for several moments.

"What happened, Prometheus?" Her eyes were wide and her voice a breezy whisper.

"My son, Carmaterdea. They took him. They are my descendants, every one of them, but he was so much more; and they utterly destroyed him."

He looked back up at her, his eyes flaming red orbs. Tiny bolts of lightning shot through his hair and beard. Carm cringed, and threw her hands up, on instinct.

"Easy, child." His voice lost the anger. "I am no Saturn, nor Jupiter."

When she lowered her hands, she was startled by his eyes. They were now the blue-green of the ocean depths, and water streamed down his face.

"I do not understand. If they live just one hundred years, Deucalion must have been long expired by the time you—"

"Not Deucalion. It was my second son. I was permitted to observe the humans, but my punishment was to do little else. If I wanted to interact with them, I must do so only as a vague presence, or through a secondary source. The gods created a host of servants for me. They are called angels, but they're little more than conduits for seeing and hearing thousands of humans at once. Otherwise, they are voices I may use to send messages, advising the few who still believe in me."

"I do not understand. Why do you stay? Can you not just leave, if you no longer care what happens to them?"

"No. I cannot leave them—unless another god takes the responsibility from me—and I would not. They are still children of my children's children. Every human on Earth is my descendant, though fewer and fewer of them believe in any god. Our kin on Atlantis are nothing more than myth to most of these humans; trite precautionary tales to be enjoyed for entertainment, or mocked as the beliefs of primitive ancestors."

"I will do it. I will take over this planet for you, and you can retire to Atlantis."

"Ah! I will gift it to you, soon enough, child. First, however, I will finish my story, and show you why you mustn't simply eradicate humanity."

"I doubt you can provide me with any evidence that will change my mind, but I will try to be patient a little longer."

"And I will trust that Justitia instilled enough of her teachings in you to prevent genocide." He returned.

"As the descendants of Deucalion increased and spread over the earth, they evolved and changed, just as Jupiter had made them to do. Sadly, they become more and more like the models from which they were created. Wars sprang up over territory, food, and most appalling, religion. I tried to keep up with it all, but the larger the population became, the more I lost my influence over them.

"Mercury certainly didn't help. He couldn't resist causing some kind of mischief, and when he got out of hand on Atlantis, Jupiter or Saturn would send him to ensure I was suffering, still. If Mercury felt I was gaining any sort of order, he would mingle with the humans. He told them stories of the old gods, keeping their memories alive. In the guises of multiple prophets, he taught factions variations of the divine stories he'd concocted. Ever the damned storyteller, he revised, and changed the stories, sometimes directly contradicting previous versions. Everywhere he preached, Mercury sewed conflict and confusion. Even now, there is no unity in the remaining faith. Cultures and societies war over their religions, constantly."

"These humans *kill* each other over religion?" Carm was shouting and the mountain rumbled beneath, shaking loose some of the stone and sending it tumbling down the mountain.

~All over Greece, people scrambled for safe places to ride out the earthquake. Many sent up prayers for their lives, or the lives of loved ones. ~

Carm heard voices—thousands of them at once—crying out in terror and supplication! There were so many that it sent her mind into a spinning chaos. Her eyes grew wide, and she realized that she could see the people now, as clearly as if they all cowered at her feet, their voices like the roar of an oceanic storm.

"I have awakened your third eye." Prometheus sounded distant and insubstantial under the crush of human voices.

Carm stared at the god's assumed form. "My what?" She

continued to shout, but could hardly hear herself over the din.

He pointed to his forehead, where an eyelid appeared, opening to reveal a third eye. He winced, and the eyelid blinked shut, leaving no sign of its presence.

"Carm concentrated on her own third eyelid and forced it shut. The voices vanished in an instant, as did the images in her mind.

"Is that what it's always like when you watch and listen to them? I wonder that you haven't gone mad!"

"It's worse when I open myself to the entire world." The third eye only connects us to the angels. What we hear and see is only what I have directed them to observe." Prometheus smiled at her, tilted his head a little to the right and raised one eyebrow. "What did you hear, Goddess?"

"There were so many voices. I'm not certain." Carm closed her eyes and tried to sift through the memory. "They were calling for mercy, for protection. Some of them were begging for themselves, but many were asking for others." She opened her eyes and smiled. "So many were thinking of others, even in their fear."

"But to *whom* were they pleading?" he asked.

"Well, to you, I assume." She squeezed her eyes shut again. "I heard...God, Lord, Father, Creator, Allah, Yahweh, Jehovah, Christ, Holy Spirit—" She opened her eyes to study him, and he smiled.

"Those and many more are my names. So many humans still believe, yet they even argue over which is my "true" name."

"Your true name is Prometheus, isn't it?" she asked.

"My true name is whatever is in their hearts. They put too much stock in a name, a word, a phrase. They have split into many factions, most intent on proving that their beliefs—and only *their* beliefs—are right and true. The few instructions I gave to them have been changed. Powerful, educated men and women have taken from my words what pleases them, and fed only that to the masses. They disregard what does not please them, and embellish what does." He was frowning again.

"So they argue semantics?"

"They *kill* for semantics. Some have committed genocide for their beliefs. Others instigate wars over them. Each religion has those extremists who feel they must subjugate or eradicate those who don't follow their faith to the finest detail." He reached out for Carm's hand, and she gave it to him. Prometheus drew her away from the mountain, south to a land of rock and desert.

Carm searched the land below. The god pointed out two groups of men. Both assemblies wore some kind of uniform, yet they were trying to kill each other. She watched as one man died and another stepped over his body to continue the battle. She felt the anger rising again.

"Can you not stop this? This is—" She couldn't think of a word to encompass the horror of what she was seeing.

"Inhuman?" he finished for her. "This is all *too* human. Even here, though, there is good."

"How can you say that? How can there be anything good in this?"

"If you concentrate, you can focus your third eye, and hear the thoughts of just one." He said.

Carm watched as his third eye opened, and the creases on his face deepened. After a moment, he closed the eye and gestured toward one of the men below.

It took a moment to direct her new vision. Even then, the man's mind was a vortex of emotion and thought. When she found what the god was referring to, it startled her out of the human's mind.

"He isn't doing this for himself!" She said.

"No. He is fighting in this war for many reasons, but mostly because he believes he is saving others from oppression, abuse, and death, by killing these few men. Some fight for glory, others for revenge, but many kill and die for what they believe is a greater purpose." He smiled again, but the sadness in his voice was profound.

"This does nothing to convince me that humans should be saved, Prometheus." She said. "Their justifications notwithstanding, their disregard for the lives of others is appalling."

"It is their capacity for selflessness I was trying to show you, Goddess. Please, give me your patience, and I'll finish my narrative."

Carm nodded. "You were telling me how your influence was waning over men, after the flood.

"Yes." He paused for a moment, staring off into the sky. "Men were growing restless. For some, the conquering of their neighbours was not enough, and they began to travel and explore the planet, even taking to the oceans. Atlantis was in danger of discovery, and I warned the gods and goddesses. They chose to move the crystal city far from Earth, leaving me the lone caretaker of the humans.

"Deucalion had died centuries past. Humanity became less humane. I sent angels; I chose prophets, but my messages were subjected to interpretations I'd never intended, and often lost. Men committed atrocities, having twisted the meaning of my words. If they weren't killing and conquering in my name, it was that of the old gods. I began to despair.

"To assuage my fear and depression, I sought out the purest among humankind, the children. Among them, I found joy, even in the vilest living conditions. Children have dreams and fantasies adults can no longer comprehend. They have innocence and hope, despite all abuse and suffering." His voice had taken a gentle, dreamy quality.

"One child, in particular, radiated kindness and love. I was drawn to her many times over. As Miryam grew into a young woman, her beauty and generosity soothed me. In time, I could no longer resist the compulsion to be with her."

Fury, burning hotter than the eternal flame, rose in her, and she opened her mouth.

"No, I did not rape her." He assured her, fending off the interruption. "I have never taken a lover unwillingly, goddess or human!"

He smiled as Carm felt the rage recede.

"In the guise of an angel, I lay with her. She cried after, tears of joy, regret—and pain. Mark this, Goddess, the passion of a god is almost greater than a human can withstand. I couldn't bear that I had so devastated her innocence. For the first time in centuries, I created a miracle." His head was down. Carm couldn't tell if it was shame that kept Prometheus from looking at her as he spoke. She wished she could read this god as easily as he read her.

"But how could you? You were bound—"

"By my oath, yes. I broke my oath. I justified it as granting Miryam mercy. It was selfishness and arrogance, the doing *and* the undoing. I would pay dearly, as would humankind."

"I restored her body and removed her memory of what I had done. Even as I did, I discovered a wonder. She had conceived of me, a life barely begun. He would have his mother's generosity, compassion, and my power. I could not—*would* not extinguish that life, no matter the consequences. The child could be my instrument, with which I would repair humanity, or so my arrogance led me to believe."

"Did he rebel against you then?" Carm asked.

"Oh, no. He did exactly what I demanded of him." He looked up now, and there were tears raining down his cheeks.

"Yehoshua performed miracles, healed the ailing humans in body and spirit. He redeemed many men and women, but he could only influence those who were in his presence. There were too many humans who were beyond his reach. Many of those men were in positions of power, and Yehoshua was a threat to their authority."

"I believed that, eventually, my many descendants would succumb to his gentle guidance and compelling charm. However, I underestimated humankind, and I demanded too much of Yehoshua in my increased weakness. You see: Mercury was visiting when I restored Miryam. I did not know until after he had reported to Jupiter. The most powerful and ancient of the gods came, all of them together. I was stripped of much of my power. Before, I was oath-bound to inaction. Now, I am *incapable* of action, with one exception, granted only due to Mercury's mischief from before the exodus of the gods: I can reverse anything wrought by any god but Jupiter or Saturn."

"That is how you were able to undo what I changed!"

"Yes. So you see, I could no longer intervene with humanity directly. I could, however, use my demigod son as an instrument of my will, if he were willing; and he was."

"By my command, Yehoshua tried to bring the humans together. Every miracle he performed, or sermon he gave, was designed to bring men to a common belief in me as the one god, but many did not understand. They heard only what they wanted, only what justified their own ambitions and behaviours. Even his closest followers clung to certain teachings and overlooked the rest."

"If Yehoshua attempted to rectify some leaders' misconceptions, those people turned away from him. His power created fear in some, hatred in others. Many sought his demise."

"But he was nearly immortal!" Carm protested. "How could they possibly kill him?"

"They did not have to. They had only to murder his spirit. As I had, he began to despair. Atrocities were committed in his name, as they had been in mine. Many of Yehoshua's followers suffered persecution at the hands of his enemies. As men died for their faith in him, he became increasingly distraught. He begged me to release him, first from the mission I had mandated, then from his divinity, and finally from existence. I denied him many times over. I begged him to carry on, but he refused."

"Yehoshua allowed his most powerful enemies to capture him. In fact, he set one of his own men to betray him. These enemies tortured him, and he begged me for release. When I could bear his pain no longer, I granted it."

"So *you* destroyed him." She ached for the god, finally understanding what it must have cost him.

"I released him, yes. I restored him, too. I'd hoped it would provide inspiration and strength to those who tried to follow his teachings. Much had changed in the way I wanted humans to live, and Yehoshua became a symbol of, and a martyr to, that change. Sadly, humans were just as divided over Yehoshua as they were over me."

"So you just gave up?" Carm asked. "Why did you not simply travel to Atlantis and beg for your liberation? Surely you had been punished enough for your indiscretions by then?"

"Perhaps, but I couldn't just abandon humankind." His lips quirked to the left in a half-smile, even as the tears continued to fall.

"Isn't that exactly what you did?"

"I withdrew to mourn. I didn't—" He bowed his head again.

"You withdrew for over two thousand years, Prometheus!" She felt cruel for berating him, but he must see her point, now. "I'm surprised they haven't exterminated themselves! Just leave them, already. Let me awaken Gaia, and she will obliterate these vermin *for* you!"

"*No!*" The mountain shook beneath them. His lips thinned as they pressed together.

He took the form of a cloud and began to glide through the sky. Carm hurried to follow his lead. Soon, they were two monstrous clouds racing on the wind.

As they sped over a city, a gathered crowd caught the attention of the goddess.

"See?" Carm slowed to point at a grand palace, before which a crowd of humans had gathered.

They were holding signs, shoving each other forward, and shouting at the walls, while a row of men wearing black uniforms and protective helmets tried to force them back. Some of the uniformed men struck at the protesters with black clubs, or knocked them down with long shields. There was blood and anger everywhere.

"Oppression and fear, anger and hatred."

"I *do* see," Prometheus hovered next to her, "but you are overlooking courage and hope. You've completely disregarded compassion and generosity."

"Where? I see none of that!"

"Look closer; there, the elderly woman." He pointed. "See the young man helping her away from the crowd. There; the soldier tending that man's injury. And there, at the back. Do you see the young woman sharing her lunch with the beggar?"

"Three, in a crowd of thousands!"

"But there are three. Three loving, giving souls. All came here with rage and panic in their hearts, yet they have turned away from the violence, if only for a few moments. Come: there is more."

He began to drift again, and she followed, eager enough to be away from the noise and stench of the crowd. They came to a row of filthy roads, where the stone buildings crowded together and a rivulet of polluted water ran down the centre of each street. Adults crouched in the doorway, looking as grey and dirty as their environment, while ragged children ran in the road.

"See? Hunger and sickness. These people live in filth. Why do those in the palaces not share their excess?"

"Because they are powerful and greedy for more, always; but that isn't why I brought you here. Look for the goodness. It is here."

"I see deprivation and sadness, but no goodness here."

"The children. Look to the children!"

A small girl skipped and sang around a huddle of children

crouched in the mud. Her eyes were over-bright, her face different from her peers, flatter and broader. This child was older than the others, but seemed younger of spirit. The smaller children were drawing pictures in the muck with their fingers, stick renderings of people. Carm looked closer and saw that all the drawn figures were smiling. One of the boys lifted a mud-covered hand and smeared the face of the child next to him. She squealed and scooped up a handful, tossing it at the boy. Another child laughed. The skipping girl fell, letting loose a cry as she skidded on the cobblestone street.

The burgeoning mud-fight ceased immediately, and four of the children helped the injured girl to the nearest adult. It was a woman. She held a cup of water, clean water, as though it were her most prized possession. She'd been sipping at it, while she watched the children play.

When the woman saw the scraped knee and the blood, she tore off a piece of her hem, dipped it in the cup and washed the wound clean.

"See how kind the woman is? How caring?"

"She tended her child. What does—?"

"Not *her* child. The girl is an orphan. The man in the doorway, three more to the right? *He* took the child in with his own. *He* feeds and clothes her, and keeps her from starvation. The woman is just a neighbour, and that dress is the only one she owns. The woman's cup contained the last of her clean drinking water. She will walk miles in the heat, now, to beg for one more jug. Clean water is not easy to find here. By using it to clean the wound, the woman has saved the child from an infection that would endanger her young life. *Moreover,* by using the water, she has risked her own health. If she cannot get more clean water today, she risks dehydration. If she drinks dirty water, she risks sickness and death, yet she did not hesitate. She is selfless. Should I exterminate this woman, Goddess?"

"Well, no but—"

"Or the child, herself, for whom so many seem to care?" he interrupted her argument. "Many would label her defective, despite the joy she brings to those who love her. Should I have denied her existence?"

"No, but—"

"What about these other children, those who halted their game to carry her. Should I extinguish their souls?"

"No, but—"

"What about the man who took an orphaned child into his home?" he asked. "He has less of everything for himself, and his own children, because he is kind. Shall I take his life?"

"No, but—"

"But what?" He was shouting. "Tomorrow that man might steal from another to feed his family and this adopted child. Should he not be removed from existence? Should he not be forced to watch his children sicken and die?" His voice was thick with caustic venom.

"Well, no, but—"

"Theft is wrong! It is a law. Men call it *my* law—"

"But the circumstances—"

"So!" He smiled. "You would investigate the circumstances? There are over seven billion human beings on the planet right now. Every second more are born or die. Would you have me investigate the circumstances of every soul and destroy those that do not meet—what criteria, Carmaterdea? What would make it acceptable to snuff out the existence of a single human being? What if the child I kill, right now, would have been the one to cure a deadly disease? What if that child was destined to save thousands from one of Gaia's unconscious stirrings? Would it still be acceptable?"

"But there shouldn't *be* disease! You can fix everything. You can make all men equal; all water drinkable; you can eradicate disease and hunger! You can—"

"I can observe, and attempt to guide. I am bereft of the power to do more." His smile was gone in a blink.

"Can you not appeal to the other gods? Surely you have served penance enough!"

"See? You *do* have a strong sense of justice. But who would care for the humans while I am gone? I cannot leave that burden to you. I would return to Gaia awakened, and everything destroyed." Prometheus tilted his head down, looking at her from beneath his brow, as the corners of his mouth flirted with a smile.

"No. I would not destroy it. I will give you my oath."

"An oath I can trust, coming from the protégé of Justitia. A bargain, then? You take my place here for the time it takes to travel to Atlantis, appeal to the Gods, receive their judgement and return. And upon my return...?"

"I return your domain to your care."

"You will not wake Gaia?"

"I will not allow her to rouse in your absence."

"Earth is yours, goddess." Just like that, he vanished.

Carmaterdea surveyed her temporary domain, suddenly unsure of herself. Everywhere she focused, she still saw anger, fear, violence.... How was she to rule this domain? Could she simply observe, as Prometheus had? Was she to do nothing to improve the existence of these humans?

For several days, she held herself in check, only observing. War, disease, hunger, death; these things occurred every second. Murder, torture, pollution, suicide; they weighed upon her heavily. Oppression, abuse, and rape; she could barely control her righteous anger. She found hope too, though; and laughter; and love, now that she knew how to search for it. These things are what kept her from breaking her oath. The goodness of some humans, despite the evil running amok in the world, redeemed these humans and tugged at her sympathy. When she could watch no more, she bade the angels attend her, and opened her mind to the voices of the people.

They came in a flood, almost drowning her sanity. So many still prayed! Some prayed with humility, many in fear. Some begged for mercy, money, or forgiveness. A few pleaded for others who could, or would not pray for themselves. There were so many!

How could she choose which to answer first? Millions of souls were on the verge of losing faith, sanity, and the very will to continue living. She sent the angels away.

She had the power to make change, and none of the constraints placed upon Prometheus. Why should she *not* repair this world before he returned? With a wave of her hand, Carmaterdea, new Goddess of Earth, cleared the air and healed the atmosphere. A burst of power cleared the waters. Natural springs rose to create ponds and lakes where the people needed.

> ~Thousands of species were thrown into shock at the sudden change. The waters rose, and carcasses washed ashore in the thousands. "Apocalypse! The end days!" many screamed. The fear and violence increased. Riots and panic spread. ~

Carm saw the chaos and rushed to repair the damage. She reversed everything, including the perception of time, and began anew. This time, she knew to protect the species in the ocean when she cleansed the water, by making the purification a gradual process that would continue without her supervision. The springs only trickled and created swelling puddles, rather than ponds.

> ~"A miracle!" people cried. "Proof that our God has not abandoned us!"~

It was good.

The goddess turned her attention to the fauna, concentrating on the edible and desirable foodstuffs. Crops the world over bloomed at her desire, and the food became plentiful.

~Another miracle!" The humans were rapturous! ~

Her next task was disease. The most insidious and deadly types, like Cancer, HIV, Sclerosis, Parkinson's, Dementia, Crohns, immune disorders and mental illnesses, she stopped from progressing. Once she'd set the slow reversal of terminal illnesses in motion, she turned to the non-terminal but debilitating plagues. Soon, even the common cold could not find a host body weak enough to inhabit.

With the increase in health, food and clean water, the population clusters spread out. This was good. Less concentration of humans meant less taxation on resources, and less energy Carm had to spend to stave off the damage to the work she had done thus far. Unfortunately, the humans' breeding rate increased, forcing her to render all females temporarily sterile.

Everything was working so well, and the goddess was pleased—until she looked beyond the conspicuous, to the perfidious evil still lurking in mankind.

~Countries still warred against each other, and people against their governments. Politicians tried to seize control of the increased resources, to retain control over the masses. Religious leaders tried to claim credit for the miracles Carm had wrought. Greed still ruled the world. Even as the poor rejoiced at the bounty, the wealthy attempted to cling to their status, and increase their power. ~

Carmaterdea had tried to maintain Prometheus' enigmatic omnipotence, but it was failing, even after nearly a decade. Anger and compassion warred within the goddess. Compassion won, but only by grace of her understanding that humans could not help but behave as the gods they'd been created to emulate. Only the humans' lack of real power separated them from their archetypes. Their appetite *for* dominance was just as monstrous. The time had come to reveal herself to the people. She chose the United Nations as her theatre.

~Every leader in the world, elected, royal, or dictator suddenly found themselves standing in the assembly hall at the Palais des Nations, in Geneva. Each of them was frightened and confused. They had no way of knowing that the rest of the world was frozen in time. Not one of these powerful men and woman had experienced any sensation of traveling to the place that they found themselves now, the only representative of their respective countries. Each was dressed for business, despite the fact that nearly a quarter of them had been sleeping only a blink ago. ~

The noise was intense, as most of the assemblage shouted their bewilderment or fear. A bolt of lightning struck the dais; thunder shook the walls, and the abrupt silence that followed felt like death. A man shouted, the fear in his voice wrenching everyone's attention to him. One by one, they sought the source of his horror, following his gaze. Their own gasps, shouts and screams followed. Where the dais had been, a woman stood, three times the size of the largest man, six arms extended and six hands spread in the universal sign for "stop."

When she spoke, every person in the room heard and understood, as though she spoke every language at once.

"Each of you claims control of your people, yet not one of you has the right. Some of you attempt to lead, yet few of you have the integrity. You have a choice to make now. You will be messengers, and deliver my words to your people, or you will be relieved of your irrelevant titles, immediately."

One man found his voice. His already dusky complexion darkened; his eyes narrowed in disbelief and anger. "Who are you to impose your will on us? I have been chosen by my people to lead—"

"*Chosen* out of fear, lies and manipulation! I am Carmaterdea.

I am your goddess."

"Not *my* goddess!" This was a woman, pale as an ice flow and twice as cold. "I *have* a deity, thank you, and there is no room in my life for another. I don't know what kind of trick this is, but I will not be frightened by special effects and bullied b—"

> ~One of the men screamed as her mouth vanished. Her skin stretched in a seamless, pale sheet from her chin to the base of her nose. She reached up to touch the place where her lips had been, her eyes bulged a little, and she collapsed, unconscious. ~

"*I. Am. Your. Goddess!*" Carm spoke the words quietly, yet they struck each listener like a quartet of bullets. No one moved, or uttered a sound. "I will give you the words to tell your people. You will not add to them, change them or fail to deliver every word, exactly as I have given it to you. These words will be etched into your memory. You will *not* be permitted to forget them. I will send each of you to your home now. When you arrive, you will prepare to address your people. In exactly twenty-four of your hours, you will begin your speech. You will feel the moment to begin. It will be as though you speak in one voice, but in your many languages. Your religious leaders will speak the same words to *their* people. When you are finished, the sky will change to crimson, a sign of confirmation. This planet, and its people, will begin a new existence in that instant. *Go!*"

Another bolt of lightning flashed in the hall, but there was no one there to see it.

The scene repeated in St. Peter's Square in Vatican City, though the leaders of the world's various religions had taken, surprisingly, more convincing than the political leaders. An elderly Archbishop had succumbed to the shock, and suffered a fatal stroke. When Carm, now five times human size, reached out with one great hand, several members of her captive audience attacked her. Holy water, staves, ceremonial knives, crosses, swords, and fists; none of them harmed her in any way. All but the bones shattered on contact with her assumed flesh. She resurrected the poor Archbishop, calming his mind as she healed his body. When this second audience had their instructions, she emptied the square, and returned to Olympus.

Would Prometheus be pleased with her changes, she wondered? Would he be grateful? Would her plan work? Without the restrictions the god had suffered, Carm was confident that she could repair this world. When God returned, he would find his humans healthy, happy and living in unified peace. Yes, she was certain of her success, and her uncle's gratitude.

She had wrought her changes morally. It might have been simpler to change the perspective of every human, simply by imposing her will on their minds. The task would be monumental, however, and draining to her power. Somehow, it did not seem ethical to compel these creatures. Free will was so carefully implanted in their design; she would have to unmake every one of them to change it.

> ~Twenty-four hours later, all Earth's leaders stood before their people. Light enveloped the planet, and it was day in every country, regardless of the clock. At precisely the same moment, each of them began to speak. Five world leaders were assassinated by their own bodyguards, within seconds of beginning their speeches. Carm felt their life forces fail, and had to stop time to heal them, and reverse it to return each of them to the moment they had stopped speaking. One man died five times before he finished his speech. Many of his people declared him the Anti-Christ. ~

The speeches were brief and direct. The second coming was here, and God was a goddess, the people were told. The laws of this goddess were simple and unyielding.

"All human beings are equal. Each man, woman and child will be provided everything they needed to survive, and thrive, in uniform quantities. Trading those necessities is prohibited. Theft, murder, and war are forbidden. Politics, organized religion and money are banned. The laws will be upheld by the goddess, and no other."

The people of the world were warned to look to the sky for the confirmation of their words. Every one of the leaders concluded their speech with their resignation. All governments were disbanded; all religious organizations dissolved; all financial institutions rendered fruitless.

> ~Chaos set in, immediately. Panic and
> fear became looting and murder, within
> minutes of the return of the pale blue sky. ~

Carm was exhausted. She had stopped time so often in the six earthly days since she'd set her plan in motion—to resurrect the dead, halt wars, convert individuals, and enforce her laws--she'd finally frozen it indefinitely, just to rest. In the first two days alone, close to sixty percent of Earth's population had committed suicide. The rest of the humans held them up as martyrs. Some of them had repeated the act after every resurrection, each time with more desperate methods to destroy their mortal shells.

Most of the world had succumbed to her will, now, yet she despaired. Several small cells of dissenters still existed and those who *had* acquiesced were not content. The goddess left the world on hold for a month, while she rethought her plan for the humans.

There appeared to be no other options. The only ways Carm could think to create complete harmony on Earth, were to extinguish the lives of the remaining rebels, or manipulate their minds to accede to her will. In the end, she took a page from Qin

Shi Huang Di. Carm took them all to an uncharted part of Antarctica and petrified them. They were alive, but unaware—unconscious. When she was done, thousands of stone people created an eerie field before her. She covered the field with a glacier and rested for another eight days before she set about the task of erasing their memories from the minds of all who'd known them.

Finally, Carm had created the perfect world for the humans. She had been caretaker for less than two months now, and repaired millennia of conflict and destruction. She could rest until God's return.

...Or not. The humans weren't happy. Their endless prayers and pleas were wearing the goddess down. They had a clean environment, healthy food, pure drinking water. Carm had eliminated disease and illness. Equality was the concept they could not grasp.

She should have expected this. The gods of old were forever vying for supremacy. Humans had been designed after the gods, so of course they'd have the same base flaws. Carm tried to teach her charges, but the prayers were unchanging.

"Please, Goddess, just let me have one more..."

"I know I shouldn't ask, but if I could just have more..."

"I can't stand this anymore, please let me just..."

"Why do you allow them to stand equal to me? It isn't fair! I'm a better person than..."

"I have been faithful. I have kept your covenant. Why can I not...?"

"Shouldn't I be rewarded for my faith? My neighbour is not..."

They all wanted more. They all wanted to be better, special, exalted among their fellow humans. For everything she gave them, they wanted another. Some hoarded, some tried to bargain. Even without money, some of the humans raced to harvest more food, gather more water, and create more things they could trade or sell to make themselves wealthier. Even after months of it—of waking each day to find the fruits of their efforts had vanished—they kept trying.

"I work harder, Goddess! I deserve to have more. If another is lazy, why should she have as much as I?"

"It's not fair!"

"It's not fair!"

"It's not fair!"

Carm was losing her patience with the constant whining. Only her oath kept her from waking Gaia, and letting them all die; her oath—and the innocents. For there remained good and faithful people. There were still the babies and the children, who had yet to learn such greed and envy. There were so many who were simply grateful for all she had given. How could she condemn those with the others?

She could not.

Prometheus approached his domain with a mixture of joy and

trepidation. His trip to Atlantis had been the same, and ended in a most distressing visit with his kin. Debauchery and chaos ruled on the gods' new home planet. In the depths of their depravity on Earth, they had been as innocent children compared to the lives they lived now. Jupiter and Saturn, drunk with their omnipotence, raped and tortured at will, gods, goddesses and Atlantians, alike. He'd waited decades for the courtesy of an audience, and been summarily dismissed with an indifferent release from his sentence. The travel, alone, had taken five years each way. Prometheus worried at what he'd find on his return.

He was pleased to see the planet so calm, at first glance. Then he realized that it wasn't just calm, but completely still, lifeless and deathly quiet. He raced from the outer edge of the solar system, summoning Carmaterdea as he came.

She appeared before him, her assumed mouth set in a grim line.

"You swore an oath, goddess!" Dark clouds amassed over the entire planet. "Where are my people?"

"They sleep, God. They have come to no harm. In fact, they have thrived in your absence."

"You interfered." He watched her eyes narrow, and lightning dance around her face.

"I have. No more." she spat. "Your humans are no better than the gods, with their constant demands and grasping for power! Without the restrictions you suffered, I was able to make them a paradise. They live in comfort, security and health, and yet they *forever* want more!" She wore a crown of golden light and black cloud now.

"Yes, Goddess; it is how they were made. I told you, they were created to achieve supremacy over everything on this planet, to—"

"To rape Gaia of her resources, pollute what they do not strip, and war with each other? They are the gods, with less power, and more greed and hatred."

"It is not in a human to be content with enough. They must always desire to improve and excel, or wither away in apathy and boredom. Your mistake was giving them everything, young one. If they do not work for it, pine for it—if they do not *earn* it—they will not appreciate it. It is the way of god and man." She resented the way he spoke to her, as though she were ignorant.

"It is a horrible *way*. I assume that Jupiter or Saturn saw fit to relieve you of your constraints. I suggest you cleanse the worst of them and begin anew, or scour them all and move on."

"They are still my children, Goddess. I cannot do that. In fact, I cannot see that having the power to change everything has accomplished any benefit. They are not happy; you are not happy, and I am not happy. All you have wrought has been nothing more than a failed experiment. I will reverse all of it now, and resume my guardianship of Earth."

"You are a fool, and you deserve your foolish humans, just as they deserve you." Her words were more of a sigh than a roar, and she reached out to cover his ethereal hand with her own. She pitied him, and they both realized it at once.

She sighed again, a gust of wind that swirled over the ocean and lifted enormous waves from the surface. "You need not punish them—or yourself—any longer, Uncle. I know you will, no matter, but you need not."

She pulled away and narrowed her eyes at him again. Her lips pursed once, twice, a third time before she spoke. "This experiment had one great success."

"And what is that, goddess?

"It succeeded in convincing me that I have no desire to create a sentient plaything. I would much rather travel the universe, and observe or enjoy what others have crafted and abandoned. Amita Venus has left Atlantis, I hear, and founded a resort of sorts on a planet far from here, and from Atlantis. I believe a visit is warranted, before I continue my travels."

God began to thank her for her help, but she had already left. He sighed, and turned his attention to reclaiming his planet.

Too Much

Another lyrical poem. This one is quite a few years old. Looking back at it now, I can see more than a few edits I would make. I've chosen to leave this in its original, raw form, though. It serves as a kind of landmark for me. This is one of the last pieces I wrote, before I let writing go for nearly eight years. When I was reunited with my first love, I had a new perspective, a new writing style and a new voice.

The heat of the candles burns away the tears

Reflections on the wall of my flickering fears

The light illuminates the pain inside

The flames burn far too bright for me to hide

The lonely years.

Reaching for the light since I was born

Stumbling away, beaten down and torn

Thrown back so often into the abyss

Crawling my way back to grasp at this

And left to mourn.

Loving too much, and never being enough

To hold on to the someone that I loved

Left behind, I'm just a stepping stone

To a better prize; always left alone

I'm not that tough.

The Unscheduled Stops

So please don't let me love you any more
You can't know what you're asking for
It's too deep for you to fathom
Too loud for you to bear
Too much for anyone I know
So don't ask me to care.

You look at me, I almost lose control
Reflected in your eyes, my heart seems whole
For a frozen moment I can just pretend
There's a chance that someday I can mend
My tattered soul.

The masks I wear are better left in place
I hide behind the smile on my face
Swallowing back all the fear and pain
The loneliness won't break me down again
I've been erased.

Don't break into my prison, I built these walls
To save you from being burdened by it all
I can't let myself get wrapped up in you
I guard myself so no one can break through
And make me fall.

The Unscheduled Stops

So please let me love you just as much

As I can handle without losing touch

It's too deep for you to fathom

Too loud for you to bear

Too much for anyone I know

Don't ask me not to care.

Minmi, Morris, & Me

Originally, this short was intended for a charity children's anthology, but the project never came to fruition. The story had been collecting dust until now. I'd thought to expand it, find an illustrator, and make a children's picture book, with the proceeds given to charity. However, it is difficult to ask someone to do so much work for free...

It's not easy being a girl who loves dinosaurs. A couple of boys at my old school thought it was alright, but the other kids sure didn't. I guess it's not okay to dig in dirt, get stoked about old bones, and still be girlie and stuff. I like wearing dresses and doing all those things people think girls are supposed to do. I also like bugs, frogs, lizards and snakes, and all the stuff people think only boys should do. *I* think it's awfully *dumb* that people are still stuck on what Mom calls "outdated gender roles." It's even worse, mom says, that they teach them to their kids. Having a mom and dad who aren't old fashioned like that is pretty cool. Having a mom and dad who dig up dinosaurs for their job is awesome.

How awesome?

Well, how about finding a whole dinosaur skeleton and spending a whole summer helping dig it up? Does it get any better than that? Yep! It gets *so* much better; you probably won't *believe* it!

We used to live in Toronto, Ontario. That's in Canada. Dad worked at the museum doing a lot of office stuff. He didn't hate it, but he really just wanted to go back out and find dinosaur bones. Mom taught at the university, but she wanted to get out there with a shovel just as much as Dad. And me? Well, like I said, I was just the freaky girl, who wore dresses, collected bugs, and talked about dinosaurs all the time. So when my parents got their grant to start digging, no one was very upset about moving to Alberta.

I was hoping we'd live somewhere near the big museum of paleontology, or maybe close to Dinosaur Provincial Park, but we weren't *that* lucky. We got a house near Aden, Alberta. Yeah, I know, "Where?" The house was pretty close to the border of Alberta, Canada and Montana, U.S.A.

Back in nineteen-fifty, some paleontologist found the jawbones of a dino near there. The bones were pretty important, since they belonged to a dinosaur nobody heard of before. The beak-shaped mouth meant it was a ceratops. No, not *Tri*ceratops, but a *really* small cousin. Like, so small it's one of the smallest plant-eating dinosaurs ever found. They decided to name it Gryphoceratops Morrisoni.

That's why I'm calling my dino. Morris. Yup, I said *my* dino! I found it right here at home, just this summer.

I'm not supposed to tell anyone about it yet, but someday *I'm* going to be a paleontologist. Then I'll have to write reports and papers, just like Dad and Mom, so I'm practicing now. Dad says I can worry about being "scientific" later. The important part is just writing it down.

We moved into the house after lots of planning, and packing, and a *really* long drive. Mom and Dad each had a digging team and they took turns, so one of them could always be home with me.

I was supposed to do home-schooling—that's where Dad and Mom are my teachers instead of going to a school. Dad said I should get the summer off, though.

What I really wanted was to go out to the dig site, but Mom said no. She said they were looking for more of the Gryphoceratops, and the bones were too small and delicate to risk it. I was pretty upset about that, but not for long.

Out in the yard, at our new house, was a big rectangle of fresh dirt. There used to be an old shed out there, but it was falling apart. Dad made the people we bought the house from get rid of it. There *was* a big concrete slab under it, but they took that out, too. Mom said something about planting a vegetable garden there, but Dad laughed at her. He knew she'd never have the time to take care of it; so when I got upset about being stuck at home, Dad said I could dig all I wanted in that rectangle of dirt.

Mom laughed when I told her I wanted to do it like a real dig, but she helped me make a grid with some stakes and old string, anyway. She even gave me some of her old tools. Dad let me scoff a couple of paint brushes, and Mom gave me a screen strainer for sifting dirt. She gave me a garden trowel, hand rake, and shovel, too. She probably thought I'd just dig until I hit a rock before I started brushing, if I didn't get bored. She didn't know I'm just as patient as her and dad.

The dirt was packed down, but it was pretty dry, so I dug down about a metre, and then started brushing and scraping one section at a time. I didn't find anything for the first two weeks. I was three-quarters of the way across my grid, and about a metre and a half down, before I found the first bone.

It was so exciting! Brushing it out of the dirt with the shaving brush took *forever*, but I finally got it. After I drew it on my grid map, I took it to Mom.

My mom promised to check it out, but she said I shouldn't be disappointed if it turned out I was digging up a chicken, or a prairie dog, or something. She mumbled something about a spring on the property, and minerals in the water, but I was too excited to listen. I wanted to get back to work right away.

I had a whole bunch of bones before she really paid attention. Dad came out to see my site, and he was pretty impressed. Mom was proud of my maps and records. They finally agreed to get the bones tested.

Three big things happened, all on the same day. It was August 16, 2012. The first thing was that I found the eggs. There were eight of them in a kind of spiral shape and they were all like little balls of rock with pits in them like sponges.

The second thing was that I couldn't brush away anymore dirt. The eggs and bones were all stuck in the rock, so I had to stop.

The third thing was kind of funny. I ran up to the house, yelling like crazy about eggs, and Mom ran out of the house yelling like crazy about bones. The museum said my bones were like eighty million years old. I found the most complete Gryphoceratops skeleton, ever!

You'd think the best part was that I got to keep digging, even when the real paleontologists took over, but it wasn't. Something *really* awesome happened after that.

We were trying to uncover as much of the skeleton as we could before we had to dig out the whole rock. I have really small hands, so I got to brush in some of the toughest spots, like inside the belly. That's how I found the other eggs.

The dino was laying her eggs when she died, I guess. Somehow, the eggs she hadn't laid yet were saved. Now, here's where it gets really weird. There were six more eggs inside. Two of them looked so fresh and normal, Dad thought one of the diggers put goose eggs in, like a joke. He was pretty mad, but he let me put them in a basket and take them to Mom. Then I had this really crazy idea.

I have a pet gecko, Minmi, who lives in my bedroom, in an aquarium with a sun lamp. It sounds really nuts, but I put the eggs in Minmi's tank, just to see what would happen. Mom was still freaking out about finding a ceratops in the back yard, so she didn't care. Dad was sure it was just a dumb joke, so he let me keep them.

For the first few days, I checked them all the time, but nothing happened. Minmi rolled them around the tank like they were toys I brought for her. Then one of them started to look all grey, and smell bad, so we had to take it out. Mom wanted Dad to take it to the lab, but he just laughed at her and said she was being silly. Mom gave him "the look" for that. I think he deserved it.

We got so busy with the digging, I kind of forgot about the other egg, after that. I mean, I fed Minmi and took care of her and all, but I didn't really play with her like I usually did, and I hardly even looked at the egg. Then, one day, the egg was gone. Minmi was lying under the lamp, with her head inside her fake, hollow rock. I figured she'd rolled the egg inside. That's when I thought, I better check to make sure it hadn't gone rotten, or something. When I picked up the fake rock, I screamed *so* loud; Dad came running into the house because he thought I was hurt.

Under that rock was a tiny dinosaur, not much bigger than Minmi. It had a big head, kind of square, with a parrot beak and a long pointy tail. Somehow, we hatched a dinosaur egg.

I know nobody's going to believe me about Morris; but *honest*, we have a pet Gryphoceratops! Dad's bosses and the scientists and biologists, and—well, just *everybody* who knew about him—wanted to take Morris away, but he was too little and weak.

Morris grows really fast, though. He's eating tons of plants, already. Mom's pretty ticked about her houseplants. She's put a few in hanging planters now, because Morris will eat anything green he can reach, and I mean *anything* green! We had to throw out one of Dad's favourite shirts after Morris ate the collar off it. He'll have to go somewhere soon, because if anybody else finds out, somebody will probably try to steal him.

Dad is working on finding a safe place for him. He says it's a good thing he has "friends in high places" or the whole world would know about him already; and he'd probably be in some zoo, or in a lab with people poking at him all the time. Mom says I don't need to worry about some mad scientist dissecting him, since he's the only one of his kind. I guess that makes it a good thing there was only one good egg.

Morris sort of adopted me like his Mom. He follows me all over the house. all the time. Mom says he's "remarkable". Dad calls him a "bloody miracle". All I know is I've got the most awesome pet in the whole world. Maybe—it's magic!

I'm kind of sad that I won't get to keep Morris forever. I just hope he doesn't end up being in some kind of weird freak show or something. Dad says he won't let that happen, but even with the important government people on our side, I'm not so sure.

I'm also kind of excited for the rest of the world to find out about him1 I won't be allowed to tell people I found Morris until I grow up. It's going to be awfully hard to keep it secret, but Mom says, "You don't want to be famous yet. Have fun being nine."

Sure, some kids will still think I'm kind of a freak for liking dinosaurs so much. I bet a lot more of them would think it's pretty awesome that I got to work on a real dig, and found a real dinosaur skeleton, though; even if I can't tell them about Morris...yet.

The Singing Bones

> *For the "Fractured Fairy Tales" anthology, we contributors were asked to create, rewrite or extend a fairy tale, but for adults. I chose to write a modern addendum to an old German tale.*

I've never been one to believe in magic; not the wizards and dragons type, anyway. For me, enchantment is found in the small miracles of life; in the blooming of flowers, and the appearance of a rainbow; in the laughter of a child, or the flight of a hummingbird. Most of all, for me, music is magic.

Have you ever done something impulsive, something seemingly innocuous, that changed everything you thought you knew? I bought something at a flea market....

I didn't even want to go, but one of my colleagues dragged me out, insisting that I must do more than work and sleep. That was easy enough for Petra to say. She was born with a bow in her hand, and a Stradivarius tucked under her chin—literally. Her parents fell in love in the pit of a Broadway musical, for cripe's sake! That was before they gained tenure with the orchestra, and her father became a first chair violinist. Her mother was second chair until she retired.

Petra didn't *need* to practice her instrument every waking moment. She'd floated into third chair as easily as a swan glides on water, while I was more like a dog, paddling for all I was worth just to keep my head up. There was never any doubt that Petra would get tenure. I just prayed that I could cling to fourth chair flautist.

It was hard to be jealous of Petra, though. She was so full of joy for the music, as well as life. When she burst in, flashing that brilliant smile of hers and fluttering her lashes, insisting that I join her on a field trip, I conceded with only a little grumbling.

"Isn't this *adorable*?"

Her voice cut through the crowd at a pitch that could likely summon every dog within earshot. It was impossible to pretend I didn't know her, while her dainty arm was hooked through mine in visible sisterhood.

She released my arm to pluck her find out of a box of clothing. "This" was a T-shirt bearing the slogan *Mozart Lives* and a tragic drawing of the great composer in a white, spangled jumpsuit.

"*Please* tell me you're not buying that." I rolled my eyes at her.

"Why not? It's so fun!"

"It's appalling."

I almost laughed as she pouted and tossed her red curls.

"Well, *I* think it's fabulous, and I'm buying it." She handed the man tending the stall five dollars for the T-shirt, and guided me to the next stall. This one was crowded with old furniture.

"I need a coffee." She announced, suddenly. "Keep looking, Cynical Cindy. Maybe you'll find something old and creepy that will capture your twisted heart."

I laughed at her back as she flounced off toward the snack stand. It was a standing joke between us. To Petra, I was Cynical Cindy, and when I teased her, I called her Perky Petra. It should have been impossible for us to share a living space, but being polar opposites actually made us the best of friends, as well as compatible roommates.

She wasn't wrong, either. I'd always had a predilection for the macabre. When I'd become enamoured, some years ago, of a lyre possessed by the Metropolitan Museum of Art, Petra had been just as disgusted as I was with her choice of T-shirt. It was constructed of antelope horns, with a human skull base, skin, gut, and hair. It looked like something out of a horror movie. Despite her teasing, she'd proudly presented me with a beautiful flute of carved hawk bone for my twenty-fifth birthday.

In the decade since, my collection of morbid musical instruments had grown substantially. I now had several bone, antler, and ivory flutes; all antiques I'd found in various auctions. One of the percussionists helped me obtain a Tibetan skull drum, made from a real human skull. There were horns and trumpets, a deer hoof rattle, and an authentic set of bones, the precursor of the American spoons. I also had a small fiddle with human bone pegs, scroll, and tailpiece, which Petra refused to touch, even to dust.

It seemed serendipitous that, moments after Petra teased me, I opened the drawer of a pitifully abused side-table, to discover a yellowed, obviously hand-made, pan-flute.

"How much for this?" I tried to feign weary indifference, as I held up the flute to the bottle-blonde woman hovering nearby.

"Where did *that* come from?" she muttered, half to herself.

Her attention was on a young couple gushing over a ratty old armoire, and she didn't look pleased about the distraction. Without taking her eyes off the couple, she grabbed the offending item, put it to her lipstick crimsoned mouth, and blew. No sound emerged, other than the whistle from her pursed lips.

"Hmph! It's busted." She grumbled, and turned toward a trash can behind her, holding the flute in the tips of her manicured fingers.

"I might be able to fix it. I'll give you ten dollars for it."

"Sure." She turned back and dropped the flute into my hands. "It's your money, lady."

She snatched the ten dollars from my hand, eager to get to the more lucrative furniture sale, just as Petra sailed back over with two cups of coffee in hand. I hid the flute behind my back.

"You *bought* something?" Petra looked around at the furniture, visibly restraining her pert upper lip from curling. "What is it, and where will we put it?"

"Don't worry. It fits in my purse. Can I borrow your new T-shirt to wrap it in, though?"

Her chin tilted down and she peered at me sideways, the way one looks at a potential mugger.

I laughed and produced the flute for her inspection.

"Is that bone?" she asked cautiously.

"I'm pretty sure."

"Animal bone?"

"I don't know. Probably."

"Fine." She handed me the shirt. "But if that thing is human bone, I may never forgive you."

"I'm sure it's bird, deer or some other animal, Petra. It's as old as the hills. Don't be such a wuss."

I wrapped the flute in the shirt, put the package in my purse, and took the coffee she'd bought for me.

"I have to admit. This was fun."

A quick rinse with some soapy water removed all the dust the flute had accumulated. After the cleaning, it was ghostly white, with a slight sheen like it had been waxed or varnished. Even though my knowledge of how to play pan flute was sketchy at best, it produced music that was hauntingly beautiful. One of the other flautists claimed significant training, but none of them could get it to produce a note. It was a curious and somewhat creepy anomaly.

"It's like it was meant just for you, Cindy." Stephen proclaimed. You should play it for Anthony."

Anthony Greco was our Composer Laureate, and a connoisseur of instruments. A small man, with a huge presence, I'd found him rather intimidating at first. He was incredibly friendly, though. Even in his tuxedo, with his salt and pepper hair in a tidy ponytail, he exuded welcome. He'd shown great interest, and perhaps a little envy, for my skeletal collection. The pan flute was an intriguing delight to him. My claim that no one else could play it captivated him even more than the instrument itself. He tried—and failed—to prove me wrong, then applauded my own performance with tears in his bright blue eyes.

"It is a mournful little flute, and quite fascinating. Where did you find it?"

"At a flea market, of all places."

"So you know nothing of its origin or construction?"

"Only that it appears to be hand-made of bone."

"We must find out more!" I had never seen Anthony so animated, but his excitement was contagious.

"Perhaps I *could* look for a specialist in these things."

"I know just the person!" he declared. "An anthropologist friend of mine could help us. His name is Graf Thomas von der Meier. Please, let me call him for—"

A scream tore the air asunder. Anthony dropped the flute on the floor. We rushed to his open window to look for the source. It was a male voice, and it sounded like someone being murdered, but we couldn't see anything. After a minute or two, I called 911 while Anthony continued to scan the street.

The police arrived a lot sooner than I'd anticipated. Two SUVs pulled up, blocking the street on both sides of the Brownstone. When they pounded on the door, I opened it right away. The first officer I saw had his hand on his gun. There were seven more behind him, all in tactical gear.

"Is everything alright here ma'am?" the young officer eyed

Anthony suspiciously.

"We're fine, thank you officer. We called because—"

"*You* called?" he glanced at the officer behind him. "We're here to investigate the scream one of your neighbours heard coming from this address."

"But we're the only people here. We called because we heard the scream too, and thought it must be coming from outside."

Even as I said the words, I began to doubt. The sound was so loud, maybe it *did* come from inside the house.

"We'd like to take a look around, if you don't mind." The second officer didn't look convinced.

"You're most welcome to do so," Anthony answered, "but is anyone checking out there?" He waved at the window.

The two officers scurried in, with two more following before the senior officer responded. Even then, he didn't really answer.

"Baker, take your unit and check the street." He shouted over his shoulder.

The remaining four officers trotted back down the steps and fanned out in front of the house. After much opening and closing of doors, and several shouts of "Clear", the officers gathered in the foyer again.

"Thank you for your cooperation, sir." The older officer was less taciturn now. "The other unit hasn't found anything in the street, and all your neighbours seem to be fine. If you hear or see anything else, don't hesitate to call again."

Anthony insisted on hailing a cab to take me home.

Perhaps the scream had unsettled my subconscious, or maybe it was the hoagie Petra and I shared while we watched Paranormal Activity for the five hundredth time, but sleep was not my friend that evening. I woke several times, shaking and sweating, gasping for air, and every time I closed my eyes again, the nightmare came back. It continued in my sleep, like a serial short film I was forced to not just watch, but live.

The smells were real; earth, water, sweat…and blood.

First, he punched me; the huge shadowy man who laughed and cursed me in his deep, rough voice. The words were foreign to me, but the lunatic rage was plain. I felt the three, vicious stabs to the guts. The flow of the blood down my sides as I lay on the ground, the sense of weakness and desperation to escape, the screams I could not force from my throat as his hands crushed my larynx.

Then came the water, cold, so icy cold as I could hold my breath no longer, filling my mouth as he turned my face into the current, slicing down into my lungs as I screamed my silent screams. I thought it was over. When I woke shaking and sweating, grateful to realize that the myth about dying for real when you perish in a dream was just that—a myth.

It wasn't over, though. Not by far. When I succumbed to the exhaustion again, I had to lay immobile while he mutilated my body—my strangely male body— with a wicked-looking hunting knife. He grunted and cursed while he broke bones and severed joints, first the extremities, then my head.

I saw his face, as he propped my head up to witness the final atrocities. He removed my heart, squeezing it in his hand like a sponge until the blood barely trickled between his fingers. He grinned as he worked, a malicious, gratified leer worthy of the coldest serial murderer. Each rib was removed, scraped clean, rinsed in the river, and stacked neatly on the bank. The flesh he dumped into the river, the stripped bones, he carried under a nearby bridge where the ground was soft, and dug a hole with his hands. All the bones went into the hole, one by one, as he muttered to himself.

At last, he turned his attention back to my head. He picked it up and looked deep into my eyes, the madness fading now, but not the anger. He spoke some more words I didn't understand, and yet I knew that he was berating me for something. It didn't matter what, because a moment later, he set my head on a large stone, picked up another and swung.

I woke again, screaming this time, and Petra rushed into my room. I tried to tell her all the nightmares, in order, but they were already beginning to slip away. All that remained were the terror, the pain, the fear; the sense of helpless paralysis and impending doom.

They came back every night after, always the same. I began fighting sleep. Soon, I simply *couldn't* sleep. After the first week, I had to request a leave of absence. The exhaustion was consuming, the sleep medication from the doctor, debilitating. I had no energy or focus to play. Depression settled like a heavy, black cloak on my shoulders, and the helplessness stretched into the infinite. It seemed inevitable that I had ruined my probationary term, and any chance at tenure. I swore off horror movies—and hoagies—forever.

At the very depths of my pit of despair, the jangling of the phone was a physical blow. It turned out to be more of a mental blow, as it propelled me to action.

"So you're just going to fly off to Germany, to visit some scientist you've never met before?" Petra was staring at me with a combination of worry and exasperation.

"Yep."

"Wow." Her shoulders drooped as she slouched back into the corner of the sofa. "And you call *me* impulsive."

"I can't explain it. I just have to go."

"Fine, but don't expect me to dust all your other *creepery*. I'll do the animal stuff, but if I'm not sure, I'm not touching it."

I laughed. "You won't have to touch any of it. I'm taking my entire collection with me. Mister von der Meier is eager to see every piece I own."

Her sigh was mostly relief.

Graf Tomas von der Meier was every inch the average looking, blue-eyed, dark-haired, middle-aged guy, who could hail from nearly anywhere on the planet, though the Graf in his name declared him a member of the nobility. It was only when he set to work on my collection that he became animated, like someone had suddenly found his electrical switch, and flipped it on.

With my permission, he separated my instruments into classifications according to their constructed materials. I was disappointed to learn that I'd been misled about some of the more expensive pieces. It wouldn't be easy to inform Petra that we had far more human bones in the house than we'd suspected.

When he had all but the pan-flute in their groupings, he held it up to the sunlight pouring in the windows. He'd been fascinated by the flute alone, but the fact that it would play for no one else whipped him into an eagerness akin to a child set loose in a toy store.

"Now where do you belong, mein freund? Tell me all your secrets," he demanded as if it could answer all our questions, right then.

Tomas and his wife, Jan, hosted me in their home, while he ran his various tests. By some miracle, I'd left the nightmares behind in America. Within a few days, I was feeling much more like myself; enough to begin to worry about the expense of this whole venture.

"Ach!" Tomas dismissed my concern with a flick of a hand. "I cannot charge you for this honour. Besides, we are cousins, of a sort, and I cannot charge family for satisfying my curiosity."

It turned out that Jan was an avid amateur genealogist, and she had traced my ancestry to a common root, many generations back. The von der Meiers took such things very seriously. It didn't mean so much to me—until the results of the tests revealed another, more disturbing link.

"You must play it for me!" Tomas demanded, a bit of lunatic light flashing in his eyes.

I thought to play *Scarborough Fair*. From the first exhale, I realized I was playing *Bridge Over Troubled Water*, instead. I closed my eyes as I played, and Tomas sang some words in German that I assumed were the translated lyrics…until I opened my eyes.

Tomas was sitting on the floor, his eyes larger than a frightened doe, and his hands over his mouth as tears streamed down his face. He lowered his hands and his mouth opened and closed several times without forming any words or sound.

"Tomas?" I asked, frightened by the balance of horror and joy in his expression.

"Es singt! It sings!" he finally managed to shout.

He leapt to his feet, and snatched the flute from my hands. Rushing over to his desk, he grabbed a handful of papers and waves them at me like a victory flag.

"*Der Singende Knochen*! You have found *The Singing Bones*! Do you know what this means?" He was practically screaming.

Jan appeared in the doorway, one hand over her mouth and the other over her heart.

"No. I don't know what any of it means!"

Jan came over to sit in the chair Tomas had vacated. She

granted me a shy smile, took both of my hands in hers and began to speak in careful English.

"You have found something magical and tragic, Cynthia. If you will listen with an open heart, I will tell you the story of it."

I could only nod my consent, and she began.

"Many hundreds of years ago, when Germany was a feudal society, there was a King, Konig Berahthram, whose lands were ravaged by a wild boar. The boar had killed many men, and nearly killed the king himself. Believing that he would die from his wounds, and only having a daughter to succeed him, he promised her hand to any lord who could bring him the corpse of the boar.

"There was a..." she struggled for the English word, "a Duke, Herzon von Fulda, with two sons. The eldest, Emelrich, wanted the crown for himself, even knowing that the younger brother, Ortwin, truly loved the girl. They set off together to find the boar, but fell to arguing about who would get the girl. Ortwin wanted to take the corpse together and allow the princess to choose, but Emelrich would not agree. Finally, they chose to hunt separately and let destiny decide for them. Ortwin went straight into the forest, determined to win, but Emelrich stopped at a drinking house, to find his courage at the bottom of a mug.

"Just before he entered the forest, Ortwin saw a tiny man sitting on a rock, weeping. He asked the little man what his trouble was, and the man said he wept for the fate of the kingdom.

"When the little man learned that Ortwin sought to win the

boar, the princess, and the kingdom, he danced for joy. He gave Ortwin a spear, long and strong.

""Keep the spear in your hands before you," the dwarf said, "and let no one see your back until you've claimed your prize.'

"Ortwin tried to thank the man, but he vanished the moment the young noble touched the spear. It wasn't long until he found the boar. The beast charged the man, but Ortwin remembered the words of his benefactor and kept the spear in front of him. The boar impaled itself on the spear.

"With the boar bled and hung around his neck, Ortwin trudged back toward the castle. He met his brother along the way, and remembering the little man's warning, he decided that having Emerlich at his side would be prudent.

"As they walked, the elder brother became more and more jealous. When they came to a narrow bridge, Emerlich insisted that Ortwin go first, so he could watch his younger brother's back."

"But the warning was to let *no one* see his back!" I interrupted.

As Jan nodded, my heart began to pound and my stomach to fold in upon itself. My chest constricted, making it hard to draw a breath.

"Emerlich attacked his brother!" I hissed. "He hit him, then stabbed him with the spear."

Jan and Tomas stared at me in growing horror as I detailed the rest of my nightmares, but I could sense no disbelief.

When I had finished, Tomas pressed one hand to his chest, as if to keep his heart in place. Jan shuddered, one great physical motion that ran like a wave from her head to her feet.

"Emerlich took the boar to the konig, and wed the daughter, becoming next in line for the throne. He told everyone that the boar must have killed Ortwin, as he had found it covered in blood already. For many years, the people believed him.

"To Emerlich's dismay, Konig Berahthram recovered from his wounds. Emerlich chafed at having to wait for his kingdom, but he played the dutiful son-in-law. His own sons grew. One would be konig after Emerlich, the second would be his..." she groped for the right word, "his chamberlain. The third, the youngest boy, being a simpler man, became a musicker...a minstrel, and traveled the world.

"One day, when the youngest boy, Chlodovech, was returning home for a visit, he was crossing a bridge, and saw something gleaming white in the water below. He climbed down the bank to the stream, where he found seven bones.

"Chlodovech sat down upon the bank and carved the bones into flute he had learned of in Griechenland."

"The pan flute!" Tomas shouted, finding his voice again. "He named it *The Singing Bones*, because it sang to him when he played it. Not just an instrument's voice, but it sang with a man's voice, Ortwin's voice."

"Chlodovech took his new instrument to the castle," Tomas took up the tale, "to play for the Konig, and when he played, the voice came forth with the same words you heard just now: ' Ach! Du liebes musicker, du blasen auf meinem knochlen. Mein brüder mich erschlugen unter die brücke begruben, um das wilde schwein für die königs töchter.'"

"Oh, dear musician," Jan translated. "You are blowing on my bones. My brother struck me dead, and buried me beneath the bridge, to get the wild boar for the daughter of the king."

"Konig Berahthram heard these words, and Emerlich heard them. The elder brother knew he had been found out, and pleaded for his life. The king's daughter, however, was heartbroken, for she had loved Ortwin, but never Emerlich.

"Ortwin's bones were retrieved, and the stream became a river again. The king had the elder brother tied up in a sack and drown in the river. Ortwin became a local Saint, and his bones were buried on holy ground, including the flute."

I stared at the flute in my hands, with a jumbled mixture of horror and wonder. I'd never believed in magic, or fairy tales. Now both lay in my lap, and everything I thought I knew had been turned on its head.

"So how did the flute end up in a drawer in an American flea market? How did it make its way to me, and finally to you, who are probably the only people on the planet who know its history?"

"We are not the only ones who know *The Singing Bones*." Jan nodded sagely. "The Brothers Grimm heard the tale many years ago, though they believed it was a fairy story, and changed it somewhat before they gave it to the world."

"And your government, or someone in it, knows the true story, as does ours." Tomas added, putting a hand on the shoulder of his wife. She gave him a sad smile, over her shoulder, and covered his hand with her own.

"How...?" I couldn't form the question clearly, but I didn't have to.

Jan looked a question at Tomas, who nodded back with his lips drawn tight.

"A few times, the bones have been dug up," Jan said, "stolen by grave robbers. Ortwin was stripped of all his finery the very first time, but the flute always makes its way home again. Somehow it always comes back to one of the descendants of Chlodovech.

"It is said that Emerlich's eldest son, Gebahard, was much like his father, and planned to murder both of his brothers, for fear that they would try to depose him. Just as he made to execute his plans, though, the flute was returned to court, and Konig Gebahard begged his brother to play it for him before it was returned to rest.

"Clodovech obliged, and the voice of Saint Ortwin sang out a warning, which saved the two younger brothers. The Konig was deposed, and the second brother took the crown from his sons, cursing Gebahard and all his descendants, and banishing them from the kingdom."

"Since then," Tomas continued, "any time one of Gebahard's descendants tries to return to Deutschland, *The Singing Bones* return also. If the flute is played in their presence, and they are black of heart, the song of the flute will stop that heart from beating."

"The pan flute *kills* people?" I shouted. I set it on the table beside me, eager to have it as far away as possible.

Jan nodded again. "The last descendent of Gebahard to hear the flute…was Adolf Hitler."

I almost fell out of the chair.

"You and I," Tomas said, "are descendants of Chlodovech. Last in our lines, actually. So far as we know, your government spirited the flute away after the last descendant played it. Whoever that was must have kept it, and taken it to America.

"It made its way back to you, and from you to me, here in Deutschland. The flute has come home."

"But why?"

"That," Tomas replied gravely, "is what we must determine. Has it returned to rest, or is another descendant of Gebahard here in Deutschland, planning some kind of evil?"

Tomas looked into my eyes. I could see sadness, pity and hope in that stare.

"The flute will not play for me. You are the only one who can bring forth the voice of Saint Ortwin. Will you stay here in Deutschland, if it means saving our world from evil?"

In that moment, my life changed forever; all because I'd bought something for ten dollars at a flea market.

That Boy

A writer friend was putting together an anthology, with the proceeds to go to an anti-bullying project. I happened to have the bones of a flash fiction free-write. This one cuts close, for me; a fictional rendering of a rea- life experience.

I thought of him tonight

Isn't it strange how memories creep up and grab you when you're not expecting them? How long has it been? ...Wow, twenty-six years.

I don't remember his name; another injustice, all these years later. I did him many. We had a spare class together, always in the school cafeteria.

He was country when country wasn't cool. Someone sang that once, right? I don't remember who. Maybe it was for him.

He was strange, that boy. It wasn't just the music; he didn't do well in school, hardly spoke. When he did speak, he always stood a little too close—and talked to your shoes. When he spoke up for himself, to the others, he'd get a manic look in his eye.

He never bent; wore his cowboy hat and boots to school; played Anne Murray, The Judds, and Randy Travis on his boom box. He greeted everyone with a "Howdy" and a smile. The bullies never touched him. Words and laughter were weapons enough. They had sharper edges than the wielders knew. He never bent— never once—,but he broke. He more than broke; he shattered all at once, like there was a fracture no one had noticed.

I knew it right away. He never missed a day; never skipped a class. When he didn't show up that day, I went to the office. They wouldn't tell me, but I knew. There were too many sad faces and guilty eyes.

"We all should have known," the looks said.

"Why isn't the flag at half-mast?" I wanted to know.

"His parents didn't want it." They replied.

No one cared, they thought. But someone *did* care; I cared. Too late, but I cared. A few others cared too. Some of us cried; too little, too late.

What did I ever give him before he tied those knots? Nothing. It wouldn't have taken much, would it? A few words?

Four words to a bully: 'just leave him alone'? I wouldn't paint a target on my own back for him, though I had for others.

Three words of support: 'good for you'?

Two: 'stay strong'?

Or better: 'I'm here'?

What words could I give his parents? Could I say anything that would help?

No. Nothing to erase what they saw; nothing to take away the agony of cutting him down. He was their baby boy once. I could give them my silence. It was all I'd given him.

No. Not quite. I'd given him two words a day. Two words: "Hello, Earl."

Earl. That was his name.

Good-bye, Earl. Maybe they'd write a new song for you. You earned that. That and two more words, inadequate as they are:

"I'm sorry.

Moving On

Written specifically for this collection, this piece is extremely personal. I wanted to write a story reflecting the end of a relationship; fitting, I thought, for the last story in the project. The characters and circumstances in the story are completely fictitious. The emotions in the story are very much my own, dredged from the more dismal corners of memory.

It doesn't matter why it ended, or even how. What matters now—right this moment, as I sit among the wreckage—is that it did.

I'm sitting on one of the last boxes. The rest are crammed into the car so tight, I'm not sure I can fit any more in. I can't make myself get up and walk to the door right now. Every footstep on the hardwood echoes and the echoes hurt. I'm emptier than the house, more overwhelmed than my car. I don't know whether I'll explode or implode. Ten years of my life, and it almost fits in a single carload.

There's a coffee mug in my hands; empty. I've been turning it over and over, looking for the places where I glued it back together. It hasn't held liquid since I tried to fix it. I'm tempted to keep it; a mnemonic, the perfect symbol of my marriage. We'd had our first big fight about this stupid mug. It was part of a set of tableware we'd been given as a wedding gift. The mug had slipped out of my hands while I was washing dishes. When Justin heard it smash on the tile, he'd rushed into the room. Rather than being concerned if I'd been cut, he was frustrated by my carelessness. He was irrationally angry about the chip in the floor tile and my "ruining the set."

I'd carefully collected the eight pieces of the mug, tears of frustration and anger trickling to my chin. Justin never saw a single tear, though. With my head down, I'd kept him from seeing and refused to talk to him for the next three hours, so he wouldn't hear them in my voice. I'd repaired the mug with ceramic glue. There was one minuscule piece from the ring, on the bottom, missing. Though the fissures were hard to spot, they were still there. The structural integrity of the mug was compromised.

I'd tried to spread the glue evenly, but there are always tiny air bubbles you miss; places where the glue doesn't bond to the ceramic. Marriage counseling is like glue. Sometimes little things are missed. Tiny issues that, alone, really shouldn't signify, but when they're added up, they weaken our bond. The mug was shattered in one climactic event, though. It had been whole, complete, before I dropped it. Justin and I were already beginning to crack before our big drop. Not such a perfect symbol after all, perhaps.

The past two months have been worse than hell. It's not easy, being trapped in a house with someone you still love, but can't stand. Even more difficult, is the sorting. A gift from his mother, to me, became a power struggle. Old printed photos were a three-day war. In the end, the truce was called. The furniture and appliances were sold to pay for the divorce. All the equity in the house barely covered the debts, with just enough left over for each of us to pay first and last on our new apartments. Financially, I'm in a worse state than when I finished college. Emotionally, I'm completely lost. I wanted to curl up in a foetal position, right here on the floor, slowly fading away until I just *poof* out of existence.

Last night, we held a ceremony. It was supposed to give us closure. When I lit the bonfire, I felt empowered. We watched the things neither of us wanted burn; the love letters I'd written him, the jewelry box he'd built for me, and my wedding dress in its prettily sealed box. It was supposed to be liberating. When the flames were high, Justin added the wedding license. I couldn't keep the tears away. He started to put his arm around me, a gesture of comfort and affection. I spun away. It wasn't the loss of us that hurt so much; it was the crushing sense of failure. At 30 years of age, I have nothing to show for the life I've lived but the wedding band he returned to me, a clunky old car full of assorted odds and ends, and a shattered heart.

I was about to move into a dingy basement apartment filled with thrift store furniture. Three days of cleaning had done nothing to diminish the stench of the previous tenant's three cats. I had no phone, no cable, and no internet. Work is my only link to the outside world now, but I don't even want that much. I'd give up all the material "things," if I could somehow get past the feeling of helplessness.

It's like those dreams where you sense that all-consuming, evil monster creeping up behind you. You know you have to run, but your feet are heavier than lead blocks, and safety keeps moving farther away. Failure is inevitable. It's going to swallow you up. The screams get tangled in your throat. Your heart is ready to explode. Everyone around is oblivious to the danger. Then, you realize...you ARE the monster!

That's not quite right. It takes two to make a marriage, and two to break it. No matter who fired the final shot, we are both guilty of the murder, and we're both victims. I wish I'd been more observant. Perhaps I'd have seen the first weaknesses develop. Maybe I could have saved us if I'd just...I don't know. There's no way to finish that sentence. I've replayed everything I can remember of the ten years I've been with Justin over and over in my mind. I've dissected every memory, every conversation, every gesture and every look. I keep telling myself there must have been a warning somewhere. There must have been some minuscule thing I missed at the time; anything that would have told me we were headed for this. If there was, I can't figure it out.

A fly is buzzing around my head, reminding me the door is propped open. A glance at my watch tells me I have two hours to clear the last few boxes from the house before the new owners officially take possession. I'm tempted to just leave them. Would anyone care if I just left them here, left the car in the drive and walked away from it all?

I pack the mug into the last box. I wish I could pack the self-pity in there with it. I'm only thirty years old, after all. Right now, the next forty years look like a waiting torture chamber, specifically designed to draw out my pain as long as possible. I wish I could look at them as a pending adventure. Maybe I will, after I've gotten beyond the alternating pain and somewhat numb shock, but for now, I prefer to wallow a bit longer.

Once I've crammed the rest of the boxes into the car, I walk back into the middle of the living room. This is the spot Twenty-year-old-me stood in, just a week after the wedding, holding Justin's hand. Right here is where she fell in love with this house. She whispered giddily, "And they all lived happily ever after."

Walking to the front door is more draining than running a marathon. Turning the lock seems to take forever. Before I close the door for the last time, thirty-year-old-me stage whispers, "The End."

Last Stop…

…Reality and Normalcy. Please be sure to collect all your belongings before exiting and kindly watch your step. Thank you so much for traveling with me; for exploring a few of the random stops by my many trains of thought. I'm sorry the journey was so short, but hopefully each of you found something in it to make the fare worthwhile. The station is always busy, but if you are on one of the many social networks out there, you can always stop in to visit.

I can be found online at:

Twitter™: http://www.twitter.com/SinMacD,

Facebook™: http://www.facebook.com/SinMacD.writer,

Google +™:

http://plus.google.com/107511848516702489145,

Goodreads™:

http://www.goodreads.com/user/show/5582346-sinead-macdughlas

Please drop by the website, www.author.sinmacd.ca, for more about current and upcoming projects. Send me a feedback message. Let me know if *The Unscheduled Stops* has been a journey you might like to take again. I'd love to hear from each of you…

Sinead

The Scheduled Stops – Bonus Material

Most of my writing time is focused on the planned pieces of work; the scheduled stops, you might say, though they don't always stick to the schedule. Often they refuse to stick to the planned route, as well. These are stories that can't be told in a few pages. In fact, Parting Burden—the third sample offered in this section—began as a short story, written for a charity anthology, early in my publishing career. It has since evolved into a whopping four hundred and fifty-eight page novel.

If you'd like to know more about these works, please look for them on Amazon, but first, enjoy the following samples…

The Scheduled Stops

ISBN# 978-0-9878618-6-3

Edited by: Simon Marshall-Jones

Cover Art by: Dave J. Ford

Learn To Love Me

Chapter 1

Thursday, August 10th, 1995

The smell of sweat, stale cigarettes and burnt coffee was like a threadbare blanket, the kind you toss on the end of the sofa and forget yet on a cold evening, it suddenly becomes a comforting treasure. Most of the time, I detested the cloud of smoke hovering just below the ancient ceiling fans that hadn't spun in a decade. I hated the way the scent of the place crept into my clothes and clung, with the tenacity of a dense ex-boyfriend, long after I left the office. Though I loved my job, I usually dreaded my little corner of the newsroom. Today it was a haven where I could flee the tension at home. At least, it should have been a haven.

As journalists, death, destruction and misery were supposed to be things we wrote about; vague demons lurking in the periphery of our daily lives without marking us. Seldom did we allow a story to do more than scratch the surface of our psyche. In the darkest corners of our minds, we surely knew we couldn't remain untouched forever.

"Hey, Emily," John called out from the sports desk.

"Jeez, The Kid finally got here on time!" Stan's raspy baritone rolled through the office. The sight of a half a dozen Kilroys suddenly popping up above the bulky computer monitors scattered throughout the room would normally have embarrassed me. Today,

I was forced to stifle a laugh as a giddy sense of relief overwhelmed me. I practically skipped to my desk, situated directly in the centre of the dingy cloud of cigarette smoke.

"Jeez," I echoed, "are you still breathin' Stan? Haven't those cancer sticks got you yet?"

He was a permanent fixture at the paper, a lifer. In his prime he'd been a 'brilliant journalist bestowing his talent on an undeserving small-time snot rag.' His description, not mine. It may have been crude and egocentric, but it was apt, nonetheless. Nowadays, he wrote chirpy columns about seniors groups and crusty tirades against the 'ungrateful youngsters, ruining the world with their damned pop culture!'

Stan's desk was where the miasma originated. Though the *Smoking in the Workplace Act* had been in force in Ontario for five years, no one was about to tell him to step outside to satisfy his addiction. Everyone complained and made flippant remarks about his imminent lung cancer, but we were truly in awe of Stanley Willems.

If the reporters' grudging respect for him didn't keep them from taking their complaints beyond teasing, self-preservation provided the extra incentive. His wits were still sharp and quick, and his tongue had been known to reduce grown men to quivering children in less than three sentences. Everyone on staff kept an unspoken pact to drink his half-charred, Columbian sludge with a cheerful smile, work with the windows open year 'round and tune out the clacking of the keys on his old, electric typewriter.

Our shared, often paired position as human interest columnists gave us a unique relationship which would never have developed outside the newsroom. He was my mentor, and oddly, a friend.

"How goes the battle, Kid?" Stan didn't look up from his frantic typing. A pen hung out of his full-lipped mouth like a cigarillo and he was chewing viciously on the end of it.

"I'm in full retreat," I admitted.

"Humph! Man's an idiot."

When he spat out the mangled pen and reached for his cigarettes I cringed in reflex. The unreliable police scanner, in its corner beside the coffee maker, chose that instant to start working.

The opening static always startled me. It crackled like a demented popcorn machine. "… confirmed ten thirty-four. … No sign of ten eighty-three. … Subject is Brandi Millord. … That's Bravo, Romeo, Alpha, November, Delta, …" The voice was rendered inaudible by continued static.

My lungs seized. I was at my little bulletin board before the officer finished spelling, feverishly scanning the 'ten code' list Stan had typed out for me.

"India, Mike, India, Lima, … Lima, Oscar, Romeo, Delta. Aged"—the voice on the scanner paused.—"seventeen. Wearing…"

Stan had stopped typing and everyone in the room froze, straining to hear the officer's description. The blood pounded in my skull as I redoubled my efforts to find the correct code.

More crackling.

"Dark-red shirt, blue jeans, white runners. ... Hair, reddish-brown, ... eyes, blue. ..."

I finally found the codes, and they broke my heart: ten thirty-four, missing person; ten eighty-three, break and enter.

"One identifier: ... a small strawberry birthmark on the back of the neck. ... Last seen twenty-three hundred ... night before last. ... I'm gonna ten twenty-five the rest." Another blast of static signalled the sign off.

"Ten four, unit thirty-six, ... ten nineteen," a female voice responded.

I turned back to my list as the office erupted. Ten twenty-five, report in person; ten nineteen, return to the department.

"Haven't you memorized that list yet, Kid?" Stan hissed at me as he exhaled. "You're never gonna make a news reporter if you don't use the tools right. You're not gonna get promoted by batting those emerald eyes at the Chief, Em. Little girl looks work against you on news, dammit. The brass needs to know *you* know your stuff."

It felt like it took forever to swivel my chair to face him. His cheap reading glasses perched low on his nose, so he could glare at me over the rims.

"Christ on a cross, Em! You're white as a ghost! Aw crud, Kid, you know that girl?"

"My first article." My voice echoed in my head like I was talking into a tin can. "She was my subject."

"I thought her last name was Bailey?" Stan shot back. He was blessed with an amazing memory.

"It was. Her step dad was Millord, but he was starting the adoption process when I interviewed them." I was grateful for the questions. They gave me something to cling to as I dragged myself out of the shock and back to journalistic detachment.

"Damn! That's right, I should've remembered: Garry Millord." He stabbed out the cigarette half finished, with his long thin fingers. "She was fourteen then, wasn't she? Musical prodigy, volunteered at the community centre teaching kids to play piano?"

The door to the editor's office flew open. "Right, I want somebody on this one, *now!*" Marcus shouted into the newsroom, "Background, picture, full report from the cops!" His sharp grey eyes scanned the room for Beth Green, our small-time excuse for a police liaison. When he didn't find her, he pinched the bridge of his aquiline nose and squeezed his eyes shut.

"The Kid's got background covered, Chief!" Stan hollered back. "Pull her first column: Brandi Bailey. It's the same girl, three years ago."

It never bothered me when Stan called me Kid. A couple of the senior reporters resented me, because I hadn't achieved my degree in journalism. On their nastier days, they implied that I'd acquired my position through questionable, possibly sexual, means. When they were feeling nicer, they would simply whisper about how my youthful looks must play on the editor's paternal instincts.

Stan would never admit it, but I often caught him sweeping the room with a scowl when the grumbling started. He'd never gone to college either, because the Second World War had made the paper desperate for reporters to replace men who'd enlisted. He had been promoted from part-time junior to full time reporter, cutting his studies short in high school. Our mutual lack of a formal journalistic degree was, I'm certain, one of the reasons Stan had taken me under his smoky wing right away.

"No don't," I yelled out, turning back to my cluttered bulletin board. I rifled through the papers pinned to it and found the clipping, dated April 8th, 1992, under the police code list. Already yellowed from the cigarette smoke, the sweet, naïve face still radiated out of the photo. "I've got it right here."

"Isn't that cute," someone chuckled, the sarcasm oozing. "The Kid still has her first byline pinned up."

"Shut the hell up, Smith," Marcus snapped at the senior news reporter. The editor's mouth was drawn tight, making the thin top lip nearly disappear. The bottom one cast a narrow shadow on the chin he'd thrust out in a show of aggression.

"I should give O'Shea this one"—he waved a hand absently at me and glared at Greg Smith—"just to spite you. But I need a senior staffer on it, so you work together and play nice. You've got the main piece. O'Shea; you deal with the background. Somebody get Green moving on the cops. If this turns into something I want it first!"

He slammed back into his office. For a moment, I thought I might hyperventilate. Brandi was missing and, just like that, I'd graduated to reporter. I didn't want to believe one and wasn't sure if

I *could* believe the other. I gaped at Stan.

"Congrats, Em. You finally get to put your teeth into a real story." He stood up without the assistance of his cane and hobbled to my desk to shake my hand.

As always, I was struck by his likeness to silver screen actor William Powell. He even had the thin, 'w'-shaped moustache, slicked-back hair and arching eyebrows. Stan's hair was far greyer than Powell's was during his *The Thin Man* days, but just as thick. No one really knew his age, though most of us guessed at somewhere near seventy-five. Someone had discovered a loose article clipping, ragged and yellowed, when the old wooden storage cabinets in the archive were moved around. It was a front page piece, with the date November 20th, 1945 and Stan's byline just below the headline; Will j*ustice be served in Nuremberg?*

Arching his long, thin frame down to meet my eyes, he whispered, "Close your mouth; you look like a lost guppy."

I snapped my mouth shut so hard my teeth hurt.

"Now don't let Greg bully you, girl. He might be senior news, but you've got great instincts and a way with words. You'll do just fine. Don't get too fired up about this story, though. That girl's likely a runaway and they'll find her in an hour or two at the mall."

"No way. She's not the type. Great family, nice house, lots of friends, she's got no reason to take off."

"That was three years ago, Em. The girl's life could be a whole new story now. Never take for granted what someone's—"

"I had coffee with her last week," I cut him off, brushing my bangs away from my eyes. "We meet up every month or so to catch up. She's an only child. She always wished she had a big sister …" I shrugged.

"You'll never make a real news reporter, Kid," he snapped, but with a hint of indulgent sympathy. He was shaking his head as he spoke. "You get too involved. Can't keep objective if you adopt every damned person you write about."

"Maybe I should contact the investigating officer. I might be able to help in some way."

"All you're gonna do is get in the way of his investigation. If they need your help, they'll come looking for you. In the meantime, how 'bout you show the Chief he didn't make a mistake promoting you."

Stan limped back to his desk and flopped into his chair. Sticking the disfigured pen back into his mouth, he went back to typing and chewing with equal vigour.

By six o'clock, I was exhausted. Greg had treated me like a low grade gofer most of the day, demanding I dig in the archives for the full edition my original article had run in. I searched our fledgling computer archive for any info on Brandi's family, fetched coffee, even went to the Ministry of Community and Social Services for a copy of the adoption order. Greg wanted a condensed version of the gathered information. In other words, he kept me busy with grunt work while he prepared the front page story for Marcus.

It was almost as if he was trying to punish me for my promotion. He'd always been the hardest for me to get along with, perhaps because he was so superficial. The women he dated were beautiful and dumb. He gave Beth a grudging respect because she was intelligent and tough. I guess all he saw when he looked at me was an ambitious upstart who'd resort to using her looks to get ahead, which was kind of funny because although I wasn't exactly ugly, I was no raving beauty either.

It was true I'd been given my main assignment, writing a weekly feature on exceptional local teenagers, partially because I looked not much older than my subjects. I chose to believe it was my persistence and writing skills that had secured the job. I'd begun with *The Durham Herald* as a part-time typesetter, but I pestered the editor weekly, with articles I'd written and concepts for features. He'd finally given me a chance to put one of my ideas to work. My notion for a column featuring *The Future of Our Community* was just the kind of feel-good piece Marcus had been looking for. It also seemed a great way to bring younger readers on board; vital if the paper was going to survive when so many other small community papers were going under. For the first time in my life, my immature appearance helped me succeed at work. The kids were more comfortable with me interviewing them, and their friends and families, because it was like talking to one of their peers.

None of that mattered to Greg and despite Stan's admonition to stand up to him, I didn't have the pull to do more than follow instructions, and Smith knew it.

Beth checked in with every detail of the investigation that she could wring out of the police department. The more I heard, the less I believed Brandi had run away.

There was no note, plus she'd taken nothing with her. Brandi was a mature, intelligent and organized girl; I couldn't imagine her taking off without some kind of plan. She'd have arranged somewhere to go, money and clothes for the trip, and a cover story to keep her parents from searching for a day or two.

Granted, they hadn't reported her missing for a day and a half which bothered me at first, but I realized that was more a testament to her parent's trust in her than their indifference. Brandi could have graduated a full year early by doubling up her high school courses, but she chose to use the extra time for her volunteer work instead. She'd also begun giving private piano lessons by way of a part-time job. With all the extracurricular activities and a large circle of friends, it wasn't uncommon for Noelle and Garry to miss their daughter's comings and goings. Since she always checked in voluntarily they didn't feel the need to keep tabs on her.

It wasn't until Noelle hadn't heard from Brandi all day on the ninth, that she became concerned. What followed must have been a snowballing nightmare. She came home to a message from the school that Brandi hadn't shown up for her afternoon classes. A call to the nursing home confirmed that she hadn't gone there for her Wednesday morning volunteer session, either. With only a half day at school Wednesdays, Brandi usually spent the morning with the seniors.

No one from the community centre admitted to seeing her and a scan of the kitchen at home suggested she hadn't been there, either. Noelle called Garry and he'd called the police but, until they could prove she wasn't just skipping class to hang out with friends, it was impossible to get the police to take them seriously.

They'd spent the evening calling friends and praying she'd turn up somewhere, but their prayers went unanswered. The police had finally become involved late last night, but they'd refused to file an official report until all other possibilities were exhausted. They were still treating her case as a possible runaway situation, but the police didn't know Brandi.

At 6:10, Greg told me to go home. The struggle to hold back my fear for Brandi, had taken its toll. I was emotionally drained, as well as physically spent. I didn't even have the energy to say thank you.

Shuffling to the old wooden coat rack beside the editor's office door, I reached for my light jacket. Lately, the nights had been cool for August. The rack wobbled and thumped as it did every time someone used it. I absently wondered if its placement and the imbalance were intentional. No one could enter or exit the department without the editor hearing them. As if he'd heard my thoughts, the door flew open and Marcus stuck his narrow head around the doorframe.

"Where the hell do you think you're going, O'Shea?" he barked, making me jump.

"Uh, Greg - I mean - Smith told me to - to go home for the night."

"You don't get off so easy. You might work banker's hours on Human Interest, but News gets finished, wrapped and printed, before anyone leaves. We've got two more hours before we go to press with this one. You *stay*!"

Though he wore a permanent grimace within the walls of the *Herald*, many of the spidery lines around his eyes and mouth revealed a strong tendency toward laughter. None of that humour was evident as he glared at Greg again. "You'll have to wait until you take my job before you send reporters home." He withdrew his scowling face and slammed the door in mine.

I was left gawking at my reflection in the glass window. Several curls had escaped the loose ponytail I'd thrown my hair into. My already pale complexion looked ghostly against the deep auburn of them. Dark circles lurked around my bloodshot eyes, making it look as though I was wearing the eye makeup I often avoided. I was already exhausted and not looking forward to the extra hours. Even less thrilling was the prospect of phoning Trevor to tell him I was staying late.

Trevor was not happy. "What? Why the hell not? I just spent an hour making your favourite, chicken fettuccini, Caesar salad and garlic bread. You could've at least had the decency to call earlier!" When he'd begun his outburst, I was forced to hold the phone away from my ear to protect my hearing. When I realized, with no small measure of embarrassment, that Trevor was yelling loudly enough for everyone in the office to hear quite clearly, I scrambled for the volume button. It was broken.

"What the hell would *you* need to stay late for anyway? It's not like you're the fuckin' editor there. You're a part-time gofer and two-bit writer for a half-assed newspaper." I cringed, as the heads of the few staff who weren't already staring, snapped up in unison. "Did the coffee maker break and they need you to run to Tim Horton's every half-hour?"

I don't know whether it was the sneer in Trevor's voice or the one on Greg's lips that set me off. "First of all, you self-absorbed *ass*," I ground through my teeth, "I'm now part of the news staff here, which I *would* have told you, if you'd stopped ranting long enough to listen. Second, we have a big story breaking and my editor says no one leaves until it's done. Third, nobody has the right to call this paper half-assed, but the people who actually *work* for it. And finally, chicken fettuccini is *your* favourite. Mine is chicken *parmesan*, which you would remember if you cared half as much about me as you did your half-assed business anymore!"

The receiver slammed into the cradle, nearly as hard as the realization that struck me: I was going to pay for that later. The spontaneous applause from my co-workers was completely unexpected. The adrenaline faded quickly and embarrassment took over. One person was still clapping very, very slowly when all the others had stopped. Marcus was standing in the doorway to his office, a half grin marring his cliché glower.

"If the minor soap has gone to commercial, we have the first major story of the year to write," he hollered. He had a tendency to clip his words out. They ricocheted in the high ceilinged room like verbal bullets. I leapt to my feet. "Where the hell are you going now, O'Shea?"

"Coffee maker's empty and so is Greg's mug, Chief!" I all but saluted, adopting Stan's preferred title for our editor-in-chief.

"Screw that!" He sucked in his already sunken cheeks making his high, sharp cheekbones stand out in stark relief. "Tell Smith to get his own goddamn coffee. I want background finished. I need copy people, and I need it an hour ago!"

Everyone but Stan scrambled.

"Like I said, Lily: 'man's an idiot.'"He grumbled but he was smiling. I let the misnomer pass. He often called me Lily when he was distracted.

I'd only ever introduced my husband to my mentor once. They were two of the most prominent men in my life, and they detested each other on sight. Stan had labelled Trevor an "arrogant upstart" and a "shyster". Trevor had put on his best salesman's smile, but waited until Stan was gone before he called him a "grouchy old bastard". Although Stan was certain I was headed for disaster if I stayed with Trevor, he warily supported my efforts to save my marriage. He'd never explained why.

The story met Marcus' exacting standards just in time to go to print. It took another hour-long powwow to plan the follow up. By the time I collected my jacket and purse, it was nine o'clock I'd been at work for twelve hours.

"How the hell do you do this every day?" I asked no one in particular, as we all shambled toward the door like a motley herd of sheep.

"We love what we do!" someone shouted, the irony clear.

"Bills gotta be paid," another grumbled.

"We're all masochistic nuts," Beth Green added with a humourless laugh as she gently massaged the swollen, wrinkled skin under her eyes.

Greg Smith's voice was barely audible. "You'll get used to it, Em."

I was still staring at the glow from the back of his thinning scalp, slack-jawed, as he walked out the door. It was the first sincerely kind thing the man had said to me in three years.

I drove to the nearest coffee shop and sat in the lot for several minutes. I debated the merits of stalling longer before going home while watching the faint, orange glow fade away on the Western horizon. All thoughts of Brandi were still buried until I could deal with the backlash of the phone call with Trevor.

It was a talent I'd possessed most of my life, the ability to compartmentalize my emotions or shut them down until I was ready to deal with them. In my teens, it had often been mistaken for composure rather than restraint. There were times I was sure it was the only way I'd kept my sanity.

If Trevor was still angry, he may have gone out to blow off

some steam somewhere. There was a slim chance he'd been tired enough to go to bed early. Finally, I accepted that I was destined for a battle and there was no point in trying to avoid it. I put the car into gear and sent off a prayer that he was already sound asleep.

It wouldn't be so bad, I speculated, if we hadn't fought before I left for work that morning, with another battle two nights before. The first was about starting a family. His way with small children had been what attracted me to him in the first place. That and the way he'd smiled.

****

When I'd first met Trevor, he was working in a day care playing with a group of three-year-olds. I was delivering a box of used toys I'd found at my apartment building. My friend, Charmindy, suggested that I donate them to a local nursery school.

I'd walked into a surprisingly tidy playroom, divided into four, distinct sections. Three of the areas were empty. I heard muffled squealing and laughter through the closed windows. In the occupied section, a group of children were lying in a circle on exercise mats with pillows and blankets. It was just my luck I'd interrupted nap time.

All the children were lying on their backs with the blankets draped over their entire bodies. A photograph of a suicide cult had sprung from my memory and superimposed itself on the scene before me. For a chilling fraction of a heartbeat, I thought my heart actually *stopped* beating.

Finally, one of the blankets had writhed, and a giggle issued from the folds. I'd released a breath I didn't notice I was holding. A few seconds later, another blanket responded in kind. Soon, the entire circle was squirming and giggling. A rumbling snore, obviously faked, emanated from under the only adult-sized blanket. One of the children sat up and threw off his mantle. In the loudest stage whisper I'd ever heard he said, "Ten!" The adult snored again. Another covering flew back to reveal a little pixie of a girl who'd piped in with, "Nine!"

Before the last child had finished saying "one", ten little bodies leapt up and performed what could only be described as the toddler version of a full team rugby tackle. The victim was buried beneath a pile of wriggling, laughing, squealing children. I'd been expecting merry laughter in response. Instead, a roar I could have attributed to a bear nearly startled me into dropping the box.

I was only slightly less alarmed to see a large man rise up from under the blanket, pulling it over his blond head like a hooded cape. Tall with a thick chest and broad shoulders, he'd looked as much like a bear as he sounded. He roared again and feigned a swipe at a girl who squealed and deftly ducked under the slow motion swing. The bear-man pretended to grab for another and missed once again, laughing as the boy scrambled backward on the mats. Beneath the high forehead and strong brow, his glacier eyes were scrunched up in a mock grimace.

There'd been no preventing an appreciative smile from

stretching my lips. The man looked up at me just then, and awarded me a grin of his own, so full of humour and obvious admiration that I almost dropped the box again. I'd always been a sucker for a mischievous smile. This was much like another I'd fallen for.

The man had tossed off his makeshift cape and settled the children down with some building blocks, before he'd walked over to greet me. His stride was confident, leisurely and surprisingly graceful for such a substantial man. Above the cleft in his chin, his bottom lip was thicker than the top, giving him a slight pout. I'd realized I was staring at his mouth and forced myself to make eye contact. The smile reached his eyes. They sparkled with amusement.

"Trevor Shieldor." I'd expected him to be a tenor. The silky quality of his voice was stunning.

"Can I give you a hand with that?" he'd gestured at the box. I'd almost forgotten the toys. After an awkward pause, I handed the box over.

"I - a friend told me - the uh - the school might be able to use these toys. They're - they're used, but I cleaned them. They've still got a lot of play left in them," I'd stammered like an idiot. My face warmed as those cool, blue eyes held my own. Had I seen a flash of disappointment and disapproval there?

"Your little one's outgrown them?"

"Oh no! I don't have any children! I found them out in the snow, near the dumpster at my building. I thought it was a shame to see them thrown away when someone could use them, so I asked around and a friend suggested I donate them to a nursery school." I was babbling at top speed, but I couldn't seem to help myself. "I cleaned them up. I'm new here in Oshawa, so I don't know the schools. I just picked this one out of the Yellow Pages. It's closest to my place so … here I am." I'd finished with a shrug.

The amused smile returned. "I thought you were a bit young to be a mom."

"Oh, well." Of course, he misjudged my age. "I'd love to have my own one day but I'm only twenty. Besides, I'm pretty sure I need to be in some kind of relationship before I start planning." I laughed nervously and stared at my feet, suddenly self-conscious about oversharing. "Well, um, I really should - get going." I looked up again to see him staring at me. The humour had returned.

"Well, thank you for the toys … ?" he'd let the sentence trail off, and I realized I hadn't introduced myself.

"Oh, I'm sorry! I'm Emily, Emily O'Shea." I'd offered my hand to shake. He took it in his own, gave it a light squeeze and just held it for a heartbeat or two. At least, he held it for the time I assumed it would take a heart to beat; mine seemed to have stopped the instant he touched me.

"Thank you, Emily," he'd practically purred. "The children will love them." He threw an indulgent smile over his shoulder as one of the toddlers knocked over a tower, and the rest laughed and kicked at the blocks. When he turned back, he appeared to consider carefully before speaking again. "Would you meet me for a coffee later? I'll buy. It's the least I can do to thank you for the toys."

"Oh, I - I really can't. I work afternoons. I - I was just - on my way there."

I'd taken my hand out of his, but he recaptured it. As I blushed again he'd pulled my hand toward him, squeezing gently.

"Your next day off then," he persisted. "We could meet somewhere."

"I really can't, Trevor. I'm sorry. I - I'm just getting my life sorted out, the move and all. I'm sorry. I hope you didn't think …"

"I understand." He hadn't bothered to hide the regret in his voice as he finally released my hand, but I believed he *did* understand. "Maybe you could stop in again sometime, when things have settled down for you."

"Maybe."

One of the children cried, seizing his attention and allowing me a gracious escape.

****

We'd been married two years before I brought up the subject of having children. Trevor's flat refusal couldn't have stunned me more. I had passed it off as bad timing, despite several heated debates on the topic over the next three years, until the night before last.

****

"I'm not going to be responsible for bringing another child into this fucked up world!" Trevor had ranted. "Do you have any idea what kind of sick and twisted people are creeping around out there?" He was clueless as to how well acquainted I was with the potential terrors of childhood, one of the consequences of never discussing the past. I wasn't about to explain then. "We can't be sure we could protect a kid. Christ, I should know. It's my business to keep people secure but even our systems can't always keep them safe."

"I don't believe this! We always talked about having a family. How can you just change your mind without telling me? When exactly did *you* decide *we* weren't doing it? Did you plan to let me know?"

"I did let you know, dammit! The first time you brought up kids I told you it was a bad idea. I thought that was pretty clear."

"Clear as mud! I thought it was just too soon. I *thought* you wanted to wait until we were doing better for ourselves. If you knew you didn't want children, why did you let me believe you did? Why the hell did we buy a *four-bedroom house?*" I could hear my voice becoming a screech.

Taking a deep, cleansing breath, I'd tried a more logical approach. "The business is growing. We've got money put away. I can quit working at the store and talk to the paper about writing the column from home. It's not like we can't afford to give a baby a good life. I understand how scary it can be, believe me. Life doesn't come with any guarantees, Trevor. We can't always be sure things will go smoothly or our children won't get hurt. We just have to do our best, and give them all the love and support we have."

A stray thought gave me another angle of attack. "If you don't want to bring another child into the world, we could talk about adoption too. There are thousands of children waiting to be adopted. We might give one of them a real family."

Trevor had shouted down the suggestion and launched into another long, impassioned tirade about the dangers of the world. It sounded like he was repeating something he'd read somewhere. At some point, I just tuned it out. He noticed.

"You're not even fuckin' listening! It's like you don't have any respect for me at all."

"I don't know if I *do* respect you anymore. I'm beginning to wonder who the hell you are. You're not the man I thought you were when I married you, that's for sure."

"Well then, maybe you shouldn't have married me!" It was a verbal punch, and it hurt, which made me furious.

"Maybe I shouldn't have. There's a cure for that you know."

His head flew back like I'd slapped him. Without another word, he stomped out of the bedroom, down the stairs, and out the door. As I'd thrown myself on the bed, I heard his car back out of the drive and squeal away.

****

He'd crashed in the door close to four in the morning, slurring loud demands for me to come and help him to bed. I was still furious that he'd walked out on me and moved my pillow to the spare bedroom in the basement, out of spite, as far away from him as possible.

Listening to him stumble up the stairs to the master bedroom, still yelling my name into the predawn darkness, gave me a juvenile flash of satisfaction. Yesterday we hadn't spoken at all, and I'd slept in the spare room again last night.

****

This morning's fight about my two jobs was short and brutal. Trevor said it wasn't such a bad idea to quit my part-time job at the grocery store. With his business picking up, he thought we could afford the loss of my meager pay cheque. Perhaps he'd been trying to make peace, but I wasn't ready to be diplomatic. I was still steaming enough that his attempts to pacify me sounded condescending.

"What the hell would I do, alone with myself all day? Clean the house, watch soap operas and pick my nose?"

"Don't be vulgar!" he snapped. "You hate that job! If you quit there and at the paper, you could get a real job somewhere. You're a smart girl. You can do better than that."

"Stop calling me a girl! I'm not a child. What makes you think

I'd quit the paper? You know I love writing my column. Marcus says if I keep up the way I have been, he might give me a shot at News."

"I don't know why you waste yourself on that rag!"

"I don't know why I waste myself on *you*!" It was my turn to stomp out the door, effectively cutting off any response he might have made.

****

All this played through my mind at high speed on the short drive home. By the time I pulled into the driveway, I was armed and ready for a battle. I hated our cookie cutter, subdivision, brick house with the huge double garage and tiny entrance. I'd wanted the charming bungalow with the big yard we'd viewed, but Trevor wanted something modern, sophisticated and showy.

Every light in the house was on. *So much for sneaking in unnoticed*, I thought. I pulled the screen door open and paused long enough to wonder what I was stepping into.

The last thing I expected, after opening the storm door, was to be bowled over by a wriggling, barking bundle of fur.

Trevor stood in the hallway, gracing me with an indulgent smile he hadn't worn for weeks. "I haven't named her yet. I thought you'd want to do that," he murmured, indicating the hyper little dog. It was obviously a mongrel. I could pick out a little miniature collie, some Labrador and possibly a bit of terrier.

"Oh, Trevor! She's so cute! When? How?"

He rushed over and lifted me into his arms, nearly crushing me in an embrace. He drew away and searched my eyes earnestly. "I've been a real prick the last few days, Em. Forgive me?"

The puppy was jumping against our legs, yipping and whining, her tail wagging frantically. Trevor laughed and released me. "See, our little girl wants you to forgive me"— knelt to pet her— "don'cha girl?" He looked up at me almost shyly.

I wasn't sure what to think. He'd been so mercurial lately, but then I hadn't exactly been easy to live with either.

"I know she's not a baby but will she do for now?"

I looked at the pair of them, my mountain of a man and the little jumble of fur he could barely contain. How could I stay angry, with both of them staring at me so wide-eyed and full of hope? It must have shown in my face. Trevor's relief was palpable.

"So what's her name, love?" he asked quietly and then looked down into the puppy's eager eyes.

"Brandy," I managed to croak and began to sob violently.

ISBN# 978-0-9878618-7-0

Cover Art by: Rue Volley for Vivid Book Designs

Best Served Bloody
A Halloween Novella

Prologue

Halloween, All Hallows Eve, Samhain, whatever you call it, it never frightened me. I've always known there were far more terrifying things beneath the moon than wandering souls and store-bought monsters. Shit, there are demons within a human brain that would make Lucifer himself hide in the deepest pits of hell, quivering like an injured moth.

It's only coincidence that I lay here now as the clock strikes midnight on October 31st of 2012, with blood dripping slowly from my fingertips to pool on the floor. My existence is fading beneath a waning gibbous moon. How ironic. The spirits are strongest this night.

Oh, I never said I don't *believe* in spirits, though I didn't until after I bought this house. Since then, I know a few rather intimately. Tortured souls really do run in packs. This was supposed to be my escape from the bad, mad world. I suppose that's what it's come to be, just more literally than I expected.

Now, my life drips away like a bloody, leaky faucet.

Chapter 1

It was a big, winterized cottage on a back road, far enough into the untamed brush to hide from the road. Unless you were really paying attention, you'd drive right past the entrance. The grass had grown long in the driveway. I'd had no intention of letting it be mashed down by the Realtor's® car.

Fanny *"You'll be a fan of our homes!"* Holmes was an Amazon in a grey, pinstripe skirt-suit. She wasn't happy about abandoning her Beamer on the side of the gravel road and trudging up the over-grown path in her *Louboutins*. Give her credit, though. Miss Fanny kept that hand-painted smile plastered on for the entire fifteen minute hike, all through the tour, and back down the drive.

The house was old and full of dust and mice. As the listing had promised, it included a small, private cove off the main lake and a semi run-down boathouse. With the trees and untrimmed brush at the mouth of the little inlet, it would be no trouble to slip a small boat in, unnoticed, with supplies. The lake was big enough that no one in the small towns directly across would know the people from the tiny town nearby. If you could call a grocery/pharmacy/liquor store, a post office/convenience store, and four houses a town. The sign declared it, "Bassvilla – Population: 32".

The house had a huge master bedroom, a nursery I could make into a painting studio, and a study that would make a perfect office once I got rid of the guns and taxidermy. It also had a cozy living room and modernized kitchen. It'd been abandoned for five years, after the previous owner died inside, and everyone around was certain it was haunted. It was perfect!

Some haggling, and several hundred dollars, convinced Miss Fanny to leave the sale sign up *without* the sold sticker. It was the threat to cancel the sale that did it and likely the ruined *Louboutins* that made her so difficult. There was no point in purchasing the house if it wasn't going to give me the sanctuary I was looking for. It would take her forever to unload it on anyone else and she knew it.

She'd raised one perfectly drawn eyebrow when I turned down a home inspection or a mortgage broker. I wondered if they'd disappear into her hair when I paid in full on signing. She kept herself composed, with only some rapid blinking to cover her agitation. She likely spent the trip back to her office berating herself for not showing me something more expensive.

I took the contractor and handyman business cards even though I'd never use them. I'd helped my husband build over thirty homes, from excavation to decoration, in the fifteen years we'd had together before John died. This house couldn't throw anything at me that I couldn't take care of alone. I had more money from John's estate than I'd ever need.

With the papers signed and the Realtor's® promise to keep my secret, I took immediate possession of my new home. I put my old sedan in storage and bought a brand new Legend 16 Xcalibur. I'd wanted a smaller boat but the lake was too big for anything less. With enough groceries and cleaning supplies to last a month, I headed for my new home.

"When it comes to starting over, shedding your skin is the easy part."

PARTING BURDEN
Sinead MacDughlas

ISBN# 978-0-9878618-7-5

Cover art by: Rue Volley

Edited by: Elizabeth A. Lance

Parting Burden

Chapter 1 - The End

Shedding your skin isn't painful. The feeling that the skin you're in is too tight—so tight that you can't draw a full breath—hurts. Living like that for months, while you itch and burn for something less restrictive, is excruciating. Hanging on to the old, because you're afraid of exposing your new, raw, vulnerable self—that's agonizing. No...shedding your skin is the easy part.

* * *

"The only fresh start you get is being born, Missy," Nana told me when I was sixteen. "After that, you've got to drag all your things around with you. So be sure you really want something, before you waste your time and money. You rush in too quick without thinking; you'll regret it."

"You were wrong, Nana," I whispered to the hazy sunset.

With the condensation on the glass and the speed we were traveling, everything on the other side of the window looked like a dull Monet. I would have to tell her, when I arrived, how wrong she was.

My father's mother hadn't been mistaken about the regret. What she had been wrong about was the need to haul around my belongings. Aside from my purse and the clothes on my back, the only thing I'd brought to the tiny bus terminal in Burden, Ontario was a two-foot by four-foot suitcase full of clothes and books. There were far more books than clothes, to be quite honest.

Nana was staying with Daddy until she recovered from her accident. I was in no hurry to turn up at his door, with nothing more to show for the past two years than a few bitter poems and some new pictures I'd rather burn than keep. I wasn't ready to process his sympathetic attentiveness or his quiet, "I tried to warn you, Muffin."

He meant well, but I was tired of imposing on his goodwill. It felt too much like letting him down every time I came home with a broken heart, a single suitcase, and a near-empty wallet.

I wondered how long I could ride on Daddy's summons as my only reason for coming home. How long before he asked about the wedding, or before Brice tried to demand my return? Would Arzinacky be my sanctuary this time, or just a place to catch my breath before I kept running?

The collective heat of the bodies on the bus was oppressive, even on this rainy late-May day. You'd think the country's largest public transport company would make sure the air conditioning *worked* on a bus making a five-hour trip. I wouldn't have been any happier to make this journey if it *had* worked, but I'd have one less thing to worry about. At least the glass was cool against my forehead. The steady hum of tires over pavement resonated in my skull, white noise, obscuring most of the shuffling and chattering of my fellow passengers. I was grateful for the counterfeit solitude — and depressed by it.

The seat beside me was mercifully empty. There'd been a starry-eyed teenager in it for the first hour, chattering about the boyfriend she was on her way to visit, at college. He was handsome and sweet with a bit of rebel about him, according to her, a musician with a silver tongue, an electric guitar, and the certainty of future fame. It had taken a great deal of restraint to keep from throttling her. Rather, I'd strangled the urge to disillusion her. No one could have convinced me I was making a mistake at her age. I doubt I'd have fared much better with the beguiled child. She'd have to learn her lessons the same way I had, the hard way.

The twittering teen was quickly replaced by a meddling mama, who'd spent the next forty-five minutes regaling me with the virtues of her brilliant, handsome and, (most important), mysteriously single son. I'm sure the poor boy would have died of embarrassment if he'd heard half of what she was saying. I didn't want to be rude. After all, in her own mind she'd think she was being a good mother. I'd finally allowed the suppressed tears to well up, just short of falling. "My fiancé was just like that, before he died."

It wasn't *really* a horrible lie. Brice had died a thousand horrific deaths in my mind since I'd added him to my "Cheaters, Beaters and Soul Eaters" list.

I still felt bad when she'd stuttered her apologies and fled, claiming she needed to use the facilities. Surely, such a fastidious woman would have waited the five minutes until the next stop. I certainly wasn't in a hurry to visit that filthy closet of an on-board restroom. I suppose I could have found a kinder way of turning her away. My reserve of patience, however, was slow to regenerate lately.

Now, with the seat empty, I could worry at the details like a child picking at a scab until the wound bled again. *When had everything gone wrong? How could I have been so stupid?* Brice was subtle, so insidious. Of all the mistakes I'd made choosing men, falling under his spell had been the worst, even worse than the Beaters and the Cheaters. Perhaps it just felt that way because it was so fresh.

The hum of the tires set a rhythm for my thoughts, an endless loop of bass to sing along with. "Why? Why? Why?"

He hadn't beaten me, nor had he been unfaithful. It might have been less demoralizing if he had. At least then I'd have had some kind of tangible wound to harbour, a form of justification to indulge in self-pity. Instead, I had a six-month battle with rotating depression, angst and apathy, followed by an epiphany of heart-stopping clarity.

* * *

It was between fixing my makeup and checking my clothes for lint, for the fifth time. I was working to deflect any possible criticism of my appearance for his mother's dinner party. For weeks, I'd been failing to anticipate his wishes. Looking into the mirror, applying the coral lipstick he'd bought for me, I froze mid-stroke. The tube slipped from nerveless fingers and bounced around in the sink, dropping hollow echoes behind it. I stared at the stranger in the mirror.

"I hate makeup! I hate *you*!" It was barely more than a whisper, but in echoed in my head like a scream.

Tears threatened, but I choked them down. Who *was* that woman in the little black dress? Certainly not me! The myriad crystals around the collar-like neck and empire waist were far too flashy for me, the diamonds dripping from my ears too ostentatious. This woman was too urbane, too tense, too contrived.

"Dammit, Melissa, what's taking so long?" Brice was pounding on the bathroom door. "We're going to be late. Mother will be furious!"

I needed more time. My head was pounding, suddenly, and I couldn't get my thoughts to sit still. There was something in them, some kind of salvation, but the urgency and anger in his voice chased it away. My hand snatched up the lipstick and finished the application, my body ignoring the dwindling protest in my mind.

When I opened the door, his fist came millimeters from punching me in the face. He turned his swing just in time. I didn't even flinch.

"Your eyeliner is too dark." He didn't say another word to me the rest of the night.

I didn't care. Brice must have thought the silent treatment would be punishment for my failure to correct the issue immediately. Frankly, it was a relief. The lack of conversation meant I was less distracted from taking in everything around me, with my renewed perception.

"Your eyeliner is too dark." That was how his mother greeted

181

me before she turned to Brice. "Honestly, dear," she sighed, "it's an anniversary dinner, not a night club."

Brice's lips became thin and pale. A vein at his temple throbbed. His bright blue eyes narrowed and his jaw flexed, but not a sound came from his mouth. No one argued with Beverly Towers and escaped unpunished.

"I think she looks lovely!" Byron Towers was the exception. "Don't fuss at the poor girl, Bev."

Another man would have fallen to his knees, and begged for mercy, under the glare she leveled at her husband. Byron couldn't have cared less. He'd always been a gregarious soul, and earthy. At first glance, most would write Byron off as an office worker of some sort, a nine-to-five paper pusher, hiding in a back office. A closer inspection would reveal the subtle hints of his inherited wealth. The sports jacket he was wearing was Gucci and the trousers were Marks and Spencer. The ring on his pinky wasn't onyx, but black diamond. His shoes were from Saks.

Beverly, on the other hand, was positively dripping with diamond jewelry and her gown, a cascade of marine blue that matched her eyes and those of her son, was the latest from Jovani. Her carefully coloured hair was swept up into a complex, but tidy, up-do, lacking only a tiara. Beverly carried herself like a duchess. Whenever she spoke to anyone but Byron, the recipient of her scrutiny was left feeling woefully inadequate.

I'd certainly never managed to gain Beverly's approval, and Brice had become progressively more desperate about it since we'd moved in together, and become engaged. All through dinner, it felt increasingly difficult to breathe, as the air itself thickened from the tension. I couldn't believe the other guests couldn't feel it, but they were all laughing and chattering as though Beverly wasn't glaring at me from under her bangs, likely wishing I'd burst into flames.

The ring of crystal startled me out of my sullen daydreaming. Beverly cringed every time Byron struck the wine glass with his knife, but he didn't stop until he had the undivided attention of everyone at the table.

"I have a very special announcement to make!" Byron winked at me as he stood and raised the glass.

It was easy to smile back. Perhaps he was about to announce his well-earned, and long-overdue, retirement. When Brice took my hand, I set irritation aside for Byron's sake.

"The date has finally been set! I'm thrilled to announce that the marriage of Melissa Shuler to Brice Towers will take place on the thirteenth of April, two-thousand-fourteen, a year from today!"

My lips froze, surely grimacing as all eyes turned on us. Beverly's glare, if it were possible, looked twice as venomous as usual.

"Since that's also Beverly's and my thirtieth wedding anniversary, we'll be combining the reception and our anniversary party in one grand dinner-ball, at the Regency Park Resort in Huntsville. I am thrilled to welcome Melissa to the family!" He winked at his audience. "And don't worry, folks, I'm picking up the tab for the drinks. Ha *ha*!"

The guests laughed along and animated conversations ensued.

Beverly only sniffed and scowled at her dish of Panna Cotta. Brice squirmed in his seat, squeezing my hand far too tight. Byron's good cheer faltered as he looked to Brice, and then Beverly, and finally to me.

"Good gravy, boy!" Byron's thunderous shout brought instant silence to the room. He looked into my eyes. "You *were* consulted about this, Melissa?"

I would have lied, not to save Brice the embarrassment, but to save Byron.

"Why should *she* be consulted?" The words hissed through Beverly's teeth and crept up the back of my neck. "*I* wasn't."

No one dared to blink as she rose from her seat, and glided out of the room. I would have gladly burst into flame, there and then.

* * *

Somehow, I staggered through the next three days without Brice suspecting my anger. It was oddly like an out-of-body experience. As my physical being performed its usual tasks, on autopilot, I sat on my own shoulder, an outsider in my head, and simply observed. This stranger had stolen my life, allowing it to become something I despised.

Brice Towers didn't demand, he suggested. He didn't insult; he advised.

"Wouldn't it be nice to have a salad with dinner tonight? Then *we—*" *Meaning me, I realized, now.* "—can cut back those heavy starches that just turn into fat."

I'd nod and add a salad to the menu, as my brain examined the directions for every nuance of voice, and body language.

"You know, sweetie, you look great in that sweater, but the brown fluffy one really brings out the colour of your eyes."

When my physical being went to the closet, my mental presence counted a dozen brown shirts and sweaters. He'd bought most of them for me. In fact, he'd picked out eighty percent of my wardrobe. He'd suggested all my makeup colours as well. Such little things I'd viewed as kindnesses, but as the criticism piled up and the loving attentiveness thinned, a layer of resentment spread over me.

Brice had been the one to secure my job as a secretary at the high-school. A job I'd loathed more every day, with its repetitive tasks and endless minutiae. With my background of serving and bartending, I never would have thought to apply there on my own. Three of the school board members were in his poker group, and when they'd brought the position to Brice's attention, he was determined to make it mine. He told me it was a job more worthy of my intelligence. My resume had been requested, he claimed. Brice had slowly and subtly manipulated me into becoming someone I didn't want to be. I became someone I didn't even like, but I was the one who allowed it. He really believed he was doing it all for me.

"I just want to help you to be the best you can be."

I wanted to laugh, cry and scream, all at once. The cringing, mewling fuss-budget I'd become vanished in one violent burst of all-consuming fury. Somehow, the ghost of my mother emerged from the smoke, granting me some of her composure.

"This isn't the army, Brice. It's not your job to train me, or mold me. I'm not one of your damned projects! Was I not good enough for you when we started dating? You were happy enough to ask me out when I was just a lowly waitress. Do I have to *become* your mother before you're satisfied now?"

His jaw fell open and his eyes became two steel discs. I'd never defied him before, and my accusation was too close to truth. I spotted a flash of panic before he composed himself.

"Of course you were, Missy! I just knew you hadn't been given the opportunity to live up to your potential."

That was it. That was when I knew I wasn't going to marry this man. I'd taken my final suggestion, made my last improvement. Loneliness was enviable to existing as his living sculpture, always incomplete.

The initial anger at Brice turned inward in the days following. Then a hollow ache in my chest swelled and filled the space behind my ribs. Like dark magic, it grew, until my lungs couldn't expand and my heart ached. Then it petrified, became a stone, cold and heavy behind my ribs. The pain clawed its way into my head. I was sure my skull would crack, and I would cry blood. Just as I could take no more, as my skin was so tight that I wanted to scream, a tear escaped. Every one after a chip of diamond, not the expected blood, and I was surprised at the clarity of the stone. The gem-tears fell, silently, until I was stretched and hollow again. I'd finally reached the limit of my patience.

* * *

Six weeks of hell later, I packed my suitcase and bought a bus ticket. Daddy's phone call had come just in time. I wasn't happy to hear that Nana was so sick, but it gave me just the excuse I needed to put some distance between me and Brice Towers. Maybe those miles would give me the security to make it a clean break.

* * *

The driver announced my stop. I set aside the analysis and prepared to disembark. Meddling Mama had sidled up to a new prospective daughter-in-law. I wasn't really being fair or kind, but neither was I prepared to be shoved into the arms of *any* man, no matter how wonderful his mother thought he was. My own mama would have been appalled at my behaviour. I couldn't remember her ever being less than gracious to anyone. She'd taught me, "Everyone deserves your respect, until they give you a reason not to. If you greet each person with respect and kindness, you bring light to a dark, troubled world."

Sometimes I thought she was only like that to counterbalance Daddy's obstinate cynicism. They were opposite ends of the spectrum, seldom compromising, yet harmonizing perfectly.

* * *

The rain had stopped, but the air still felt cool and damp, after the heat on the bus. I slipped into the cardigan I'd brought along. There was a pub a few doors down from the bus stop, right across from Nana's house. "Caps'n'Taps", read the swinging sign above the door. *What a strange name,* I thought. *Oh well, it's as good a place as any to stall a few minutes longer*

.

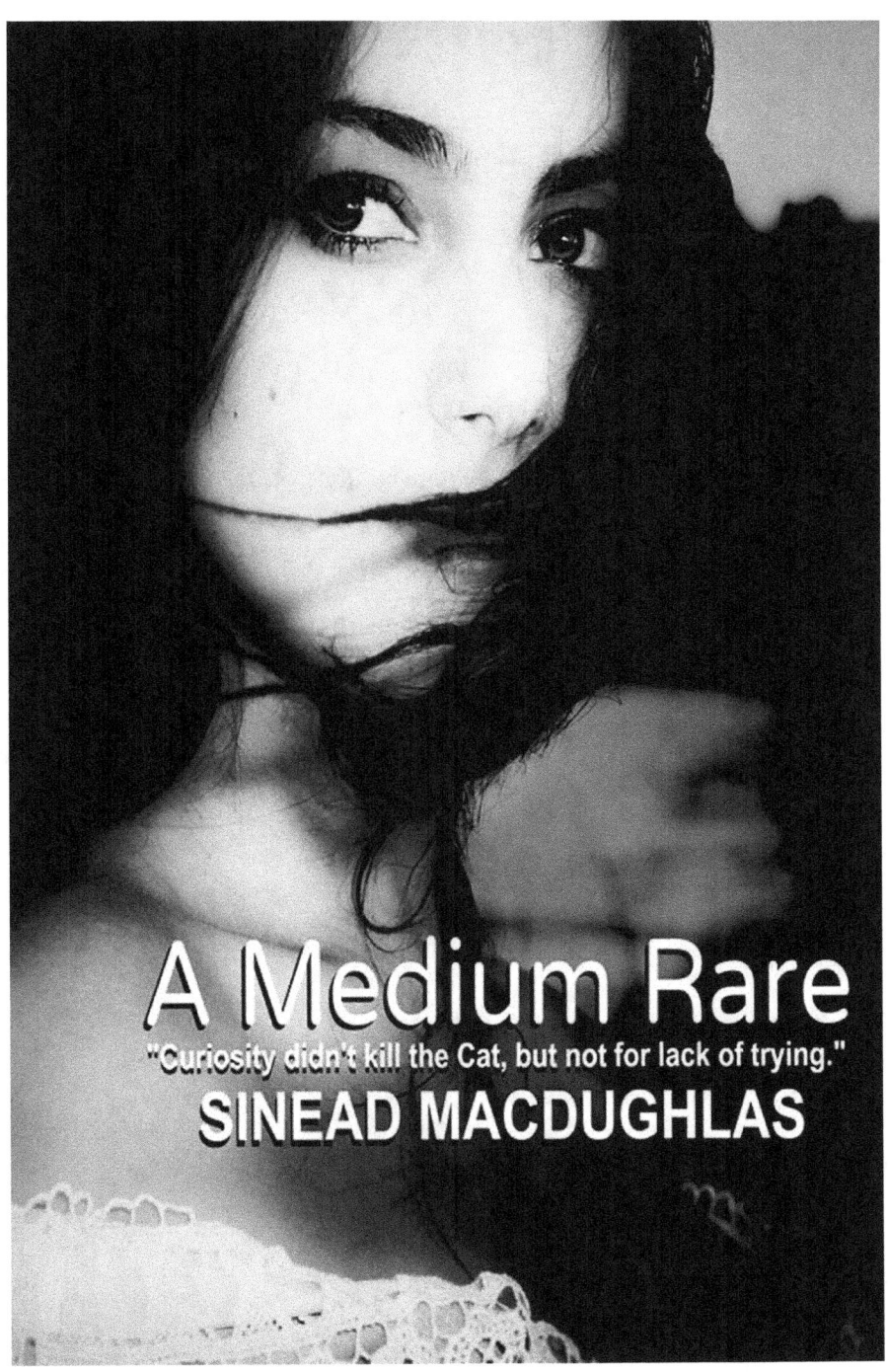

A Medium Rare

"Curiosity didn't kill the Cat, but not for lack of trying."

SINEAD MACDUGHLAS

ISBN# 978-0-9878618-8-7

Cover art by:Rue Volley

Edited by: Elizabeth A. Lance

This is a work of fiction. All characters and events portrayed in this novel are fictitious products of the author's imagination. Any resemblance to actual events, locales, or persons living or dead, are entirely coincidental.

A Medium Rare

Pouring Over Books –

The sound of a ringing bell drifted into the kitchen from the front of the shop. Catherine looked down at the fluffy, black cat curled around her feet, and sighed.

"Well, Shotgun. She's here. It's time to finally let the cat out of the bag."

Shotgun snuffled his disdain for her choice of words, but he unwound himself from her ankles, stretched, and padded through the door on her heels.

Melissa, her best friend and business partner, stood behind the cash register with a carefully crafted smile on her pretty face, fiddling with one lock of her long, red hair. Cat knew she would be tapping her foot behind the counter. It wasn't that Mel didn't appreciate new customers, but she'd been hoping to close the *Pouring Over Books* teahouse and bookstore on time, today.

Everyone in their close circle was meeting at Cat's place tonight for dinner. It was the first time in ages that all their schedules had meshed, and no one wanted to be late. What Mel *didn't* know, was that the woman who appeared to be nonchalantly browsing the bookshelves wasn't here to buy books. She was here as Cat's surprise dinner guest, and she had a *true* story to tell that would make some of the horror books on the shelves seem like fairy tales.

Beth Green ran her carefully manicured nails along the spines of a shelf of hardcovers. Only the agitation Cat felt radiating from Shotgun, and the nearly imperceptible tremor in those fingertips, betrayed the older woman's tension.

Cat stepped quietly to the door, turned the sign in the peek-a-boo window to "Closed", and flipped the deadbolt. Beth spun toward her as if she'd been shot. Mel's eyebrows rose and she opened her mouth, but Cat forestalled any questions with a tiny shake of her head.

"Hello, Beth." Cat locked eyes with the older woman. "Are you certain you're ready for this?"

"No." Beth sighed. She brushed a bit of snowy white bang away from her eyes, revealing three, jagged, white scars on her forehead. "But it *is* time. You kept your promise. I owe you so much more than just this."

Cat turned to Mel, who stood behind the register with her hands on her hips, looking completely baffled.

"Mel, I'd like you to meet Beth Green. She's going to come for dinner, tonight."

Beth closed her eyes. "And you'll all finally know what happened in Bassvilla last fall, to Catherine, and to me."

Melissa's mouth fell open, her blue eyes widening. Then a slow smile crept across her face, and she snatched up her keys.

"Well?" the pretty redhead chirped. "What are we waiting for?"

Beth's eyes flew open, and she looked at Mel dubiously before glancing at Cat, a transparent question in her raised eyebrows.

All the medium could do was shrug in response. Part of keeping the whole thing secret was keeping the nature of it secret, as well. Melissa, and the rest of their rag-tag family, were in for one hell of a surprise.

* * *

James had done his part at the farm. At least, he'd put the ham and scalloped potatoes in the oven at the right times. He'd forgotten the carrots, but Cat fixed that by tossing on some frozen corn from the fall harvest. James walked in while she was filling the pot with hot water, so the corn would cook faster.

"One of the ewes had an awful limp." He threw his hands up and his natural pout became more pronounced. "I had to trim her back hooves, before it did real damage."

"It's okay." Cat reached up to run her fingers through his rumpled hair, before kissing him softly on the lips. She knew it was the surprise guest that had him so jumpy, not really the carrots.

* * *

James tried to be supportive and accepting of Catherine's gifts, but they still made him anxious at times. The stranger at the table had shoved him completely off balance. He knew that Beth Green was the woman Cat had worked for from early September through to mid-November a year ago. He knew that whatever had happened in Bassvilla had altered Catherine in a most palpable manner. What he didn't know was what had actually happened. Cat hadn't told anyone, even him.

Now the catalyst for those changes was sitting in his dining room, preparing to reveal it all over dinner, as casually as if it hadn't given Cat nightmares for months after. Unfortunately, now that the time had finally come, he wasn't so certain that he wanted to know, after all.

* * *

Mel watched the interplay between her brother and her best friend with growing unease. James was huffing like an overworked horse, and he kept glancing at the lady Cat had brought to dinner. Everyone else had taken the extra diner into stride, and made her feel welcome. If James was so tense about it, though, Mel knew that whatever had happened to her witchy partner wasn't going to make a good bedtime story.

* * *

If there was ever a time Beth wanted a sinkhole to open under her feet, and swallow her up, this was it. She'd been introduced to so many people. All through dinner, they'd stared at her, waiting for her to start talking. Now that her plate was empty, she could stall no longer. Someone placed a cup of tea in front of her. As the men loosened belts before dessert, Beth sat back in her chair and cleared her throat.

"I know you're all wondering why I made Catherine promise not to speak of the work she did for me last fall. Well, it's because of what happened while she was doing that work. I needed time to

194

come to terms with it all."

"You haven't though," the medium interjected. "Not really."

"Perhaps not," Beth nodded at her, "but I'm sure your family and friends are tired of waiting. So...where should I start?"

"At the beginning, of course," Melissa, said. "Start at the beginning."

She sipped the tea and recognized, even after all this time, one of Cat's custom blends. Far more than a medium, Catherine was also trained in white magic, some Ojibwa medicine and herbology. Beth had missed her teas, but more she'd missed Cat's calming presence.

The petite brunette reached over, and put a hand over Beth's. "I'm here, Beth. I'll help, but the first half of the story is just yours to tell."

She took one, last, bracing breath, and began to speak.

Acknowledgements

There are so many people who've made this collection possible. Let me begin with you; the reader. If not for you, this book would still be just a horde of words, images and personalities, tumbling about in my mind. These stories and poems would be pages of random ideas, collecting dust in a box under my bed.

Thank you to my family, friends and fans. Their love and support have been invaluable. I am blessed to know each one of them.

Thank you to the beta readers, (those who read, critique and advise on a manuscript prior to editing); Laura Rodela, Nancy Medina, Theresa R. Stoddard, Line Tødenes Olsen, Thomas Pryce, Ian Ball and Janîce Leotti.

Thank you to those who have provided, and continue to provide, inspiration and advice to fellow writers; Nai'lah Carter, Wayne Pollard, Catherine Stovall, Elizabeth A. Lance, Linna Drehmel, Ada McEwan, Catrina Taylor, all the members of the Independent Writers Association, and Travis McDougald.

A special thank you to David J. Ford, for his patience and vision in crafting the cover art for this book, and for my debut novel, "Learn To Love Me".

Thank you to my fellow wordsmiths. I'm so proud to count myself as one among a community, where competition and success are pale shadows, cast by the light of camaraderie, encouragement, and advice.

Sinead MacDughlas will tell you she breathes music and bleeds words. Those who know her will, will tell you those words are likely highly caffeinated.

Born in Toronto, and raised in Lindsay, Ontario, Sin is a proud Canadian whose plots often take place in her home province. She now lives in a small town, North of Toronto, with her hard-working husband. Together, they are raising two active and imaginative children, and the cat and dog who've claimed them all

David J. Ford is a photographer, artist, author, world traveler, and airplane enthusiast. Born in Boksburg. Guateng, in South Africa, to Welsh parents, he presently resides in The City of the Kawartha Lakes, Ontario. An advocate for the Crohn's and Colitis Association, proceeds from his cartoon book, "It Only Hurts When I Laugh," are shared with the cause.

Find Dave on Faceboon, at www.facebookcom/cartoonsbydave/ for your copy. You can view his other artistic endeavors at www.facebook.com/PrintsbyDave.

www.ingramcontent.com/pod-product-compliance
Lightning Source LLC
Chambersburg PA
CBHW061157170626
46809CB00003B/1129